To Régis, who often went down the Yangtze River out of fear of winter.

Mapping the World

"It is the silent contemplation of atlases, flat on one's stomach on the rug, between the ages of 10 and 13, that makes one want to leave everything behind ..."

Nicolas Bouvier, *L'Usage du monde.*

A FIREFLY BOOK

Published by Firefly Books Ltd. 2009

Copyright © 2008 Éditions du Seuil

First printing

Publisher Cataloging-in-Publication Data (U.S.)

Laffon, Caroline.
    Mapping the world : stories of geography / Caroline Laffon ; Martine Laffon.
[188] p. : col. ill.; maps ; cm.
Includes bibliographical references.
ISBN-13: 978-1-55407-525-6
ISBN-10: 1-55407-525-4
1. Cartography – Popular works. I. Laffon, Martine. II. Title.
526 dc22   GA105.5L344 2009

Library and Archives Canada Cataloguing in Publication

Laffon, Caroline
    Mapping the world : stories of geography / Caroline & Martine Laffon.
Includes bibliographical references.
ISBN-13: 978-1-55407-525-6
ISBN-10: 1-55407-525-4
    1. Cartography–History. 2. Cartographers–History. I. Laffon, Martine
II. Title.
GA201.L33 2009   912.09   C2009-901245-6

Published in the United States by
Firefly Books (U.S.) Inc.
P.O. Box 1338, Ellicott Station
Buffalo, New York 14205

Published in Canada by
Firefly Books Ltd.
66 Leek Crescent
Richmond Hill, Ontario L4B 1H1

Printed in China

Caroline & Martine Laffon

Mapping the World

Stories of Geography

FIREFLY BOOKS

la costa dela
florida

Table of Contents

United States: Florida vegetation,
atlas by Lazaro Luis, detail.
(1503. Academy of Sciences, Lisbon.)

Where Are We?

"'Where do you want to go, fellah?'…
'Leper's Depot, we want to go to Leper's Depot…'
With what I imagine to be a smile of superiority, the Master of the Pumps
effortlessly reads the map's alphabetical index.
'Lardivista, Lawrence, Lernis, Leper's Depot. Here it is. E5.'
I count from 1 to 5 at the side of the map. I go from A to E along the bottom.
I extend the imaginary lines. What do you know? There it is. Leper's Depot.
Right where it is supposed to be, a demonstration, if any were needed, that
any point on a map can be fixed by two coordinates and that every
coordinate pair (letter and number) picks out a point on the map…"

David Berlinski

Without a doubt, we need poetry to create spaces according to the size of our imagination and to describe the surface of the earth. Beyond our hometown, the places we visit, the tall buildings and the dark forests, we know nothing of what lies beyond the horizon. There is a boundary between what we know, what we can guess and that "somewhere else" others talk about. So we have to invent these far-off places or go and see them for ourselves to discover what returning travelers have described. Those who reached other shores have always taken with them a nostalgic image of their country or a largely mythical image of a paradise lost. How then can the truth be untangled from what was projected onto that "somewhere else" in the form of memories, desires or regrets?

If people searched for other routes, other passages over land and sea, it was to discover where the world ended and who might live there. Yet, aside from promoting knowledge, there was also a need to profit from these expeditions while also contemplating possible expansion.

Once the known world was drawn flat on a map, people may have asked where they could find that tiny point indicated by the imaginary lines that crisscross the surface. Compared to the immense lands discovered at the end of the world, a local kingdom, governed by the great and the powerful, can suddenly appear very small. And, since it is the great and the powerful who financed the mapmakers and the geographers' education, how could the mapmakers not be tempted to cheat a little by expanding the provinces of their protectors and shrinking neighboring territories on the map? By illuminating their maps with castle towers, landscapes, rivers and mineral resources, they emphasized the glory and the honor of the monarchs. The images rarely reflected reality.

However, cartography has a good memory, and it can trace the progress of people moving from one place to another or from one port to another, drawing the network of routes that geometry will transfer to a canvas of latitudes and longitudes.

Caution, patience, a keen eye, courage, the desire to learn and a knowledge of arithmetic, mechanics, geometry and astronomy, not to mention philosophy, are the things a person needs to undertake a trip around the world…

All that remains is determining where the earth lies. In the middle of the universe as cosmic center of worlds and spheres? And if, over thousands of years, myths have tried to answer the why and the how of the earth, humans and the universe, they must give up their enchanting stories to the instruments of observation, calculation, measurement and secular reasoning. Yet, chase away the imaginary, and it returns through the cracks in the ancient maps, in the names of the cities and in the outlines of the countries that history changed according to conquests and empires. The silk roads, the spice routes, the paths of the great pilgrimages, the clashes and the victories and the defeats of the Crusaders and Muslims at the foot of the ramparts of Constantinople are all hinted at in maps. Jerusalem can be depicted as it was at the time of Christ or according to the latest data. The map of France, drawn by order of the king, and the names of the nautical atlases also stir the imagination. Maps and charts from the 17th and 18th centuries allow for sedentary travels that are certainly more literary than geographical. Are maps not adventure novels?

In the foreword to *Lectures géographiques illustrées* (illustrated lectures on geography) published in 1903, Pierre Foncin reassures his readers: he hopes that his little book will not boring because, as he says, he enjoyed writing it, since traveling across France and the world in the company of the cleverest explorers, the most knowledgeable geographers and the most informed observers is a real delight! However, must we not concede that these specialists are a little forbidding and that they make geography a little abstract? Pierre Foncin, in his enthusiasm, proposes an inclusive geography, useful for young people and appropriate for maintaining and developing an enlightened and logical worship of his country. Too bad for objectivity. We learn that the Niger is four times as long as the Loire, that operating a coffee plantation in New Caledonia is a big deal, but those who want to emigrate there must have a lot of resources and demonstrate that they are worthy of being called a French settler, and many other considerations the colonial period glosses over with certainty in its version of the world's geography.

Maps are not neutral, nor are those who decipher them. This is what "mapping the world means" — uncovering the buried myths and legends and retracing the sequence of political, religious and economic history and the slow evolution of the scientific mind that patiently searches the land, sky, globes, atlases and maps to decipher and to understand the universe in order to answer humanity's ultimate questions: Where are we? Who are we?

Step by Step

Daydreaming about the world

"To the north of the Far North, there lies the sea of shadows: Heavenly Lake. In it lives a fish whose length and breadth are several lis long. His name is kun. There also lives a bird whose name is peng. His wings are like clouds suspended in the sky and his body is in proportion to the clouds. Does the world know that such creatures exist?"

Mathieu Rémi, Anthologie des mythes et légendes de la Chine ancienne (Anthology of the Myths and Legends of Ancient China)

n their *Dictionary of Imaginary Places*, Alberto Manguel and Giann Guadalupi show the extent to which literary stories of adventures abound in ancient cities, islands and archipelagoes — wonderful lands traveled for the first time by the heroes. In *The Odyssey*, Odysseus does not return, as planned, to Ithaca because he committed one too many senseless raids on the island of the Cicones. As he rounds Cape Malea at the southern tip of the Peloponnese, he is drawn toward a world with islands inhabited by monsters and goddesses, which lies beyond the world he knows. But Homer is not a geographer, and topographical indications are rare in *The Odyssey*, except for the land of the dead, which, for a Mediterranean author, can only be found in the north, in the land of cold.

In the stories about his exploits, Alexander the Great also crosses the limits of the known world, as he travels all the way to India and battles with Gog and Magog, the two giants and kings of the monstrous and the impure. He imprisons them "behind a wall," which many travelers would try to find.

Whether it was Atlantis, the kingdom of Father John or the island of St. Brendan, imaginary places have excited the curiosity of travelers, princes and popes. They have influenced our images of people from other lands. However, if the landscapes and the customs of their inhabitants are accurately portrayed, they owe their geographical reality and their latitude and longitude solely to the good faith of the reader. For example, why question the existence of the "great and admirable kingdom of Antangil, unknown to historians and cosmographers to this day," according to the story told by Joachim Du Moulin in 1616?

Inventing worlds such as those described above allows one to model them based on the political powers in place and society's aspirations or, on the contrary, to manipulate beliefs, to draw faith beyond reason and to affirm the supremacy of one truth over all others. Drawing the mythical outline of untamed lands reassures everyone about the benefits of civilization. And if such strange lands are faithless and lawless, how can one not dare, for the glory of God, to convert them after denouncing their vices at the same time as taking stock of their natural resources?

These allegorical voyages, where the only reference points are one's deeply rooted moral, political and religious beliefs — rather than scientific data — have produced a particular representation of the world. But is not the unavowed purpose of these imaginary worlds to satisfy society's desire for utopias and to encourage travelers to discover their inner world rather than embark on a geographical tour?

However, for those in the West who are still searching for the Happy Isles, the answer may lie in Japan, in the tales told by the sailors returning from the Fortunate Isles. There the soil is rich in precious stones, and the inhabitants are beautiful in their eternal youth… Man may have had no other desire over the millennia but one: to see and imagine the world.

Tiny Cosmos

Australia:
The Myth of the
Creation of the
constellation Wuripimba
according to Aboriginal
cosmogony. (Painting on
eucapyltus bark, Arnhem
Land, Australia. 20th
century. Quai Branly
Museum, Paris.)

Round or oblong? Placed atop the shoulders of a giant, on the back of a tortoise or on four elephants? Mandarin or melon? Clasped by two masses of water? Inhabited by barbarians and monsters? What does the earth look like and how should it be depicted? All mythologies have tried to solve the mystery of the origins of the earth, its shape and its matter, and fantastical cosmographies bear witness to this. Nonetheless, everyone knows that the words "image" and "magic" are deeply entwined in the word "imagine."

To understand one's world, a tale explaining its origins must be invented, in which nothing is the result of absurd and blind luck, but divine will. The people who subscribe to a story into which they have written themselves can imagine their place in it. This is why their tales name the gods and assign them a nomadic or sedentary place and a function in the different upper, middle and lower universes. Having said this, people create reference points to understand the origins of the cycle of life, from birth to death, and that of the day, the night and the seasons. Their regularity demonstrates a cosmic harmony and shows that an alliance has been forged with the deities to ensure the world never returns to chaos and is never destroyed by a flood or beings from an unknown world.

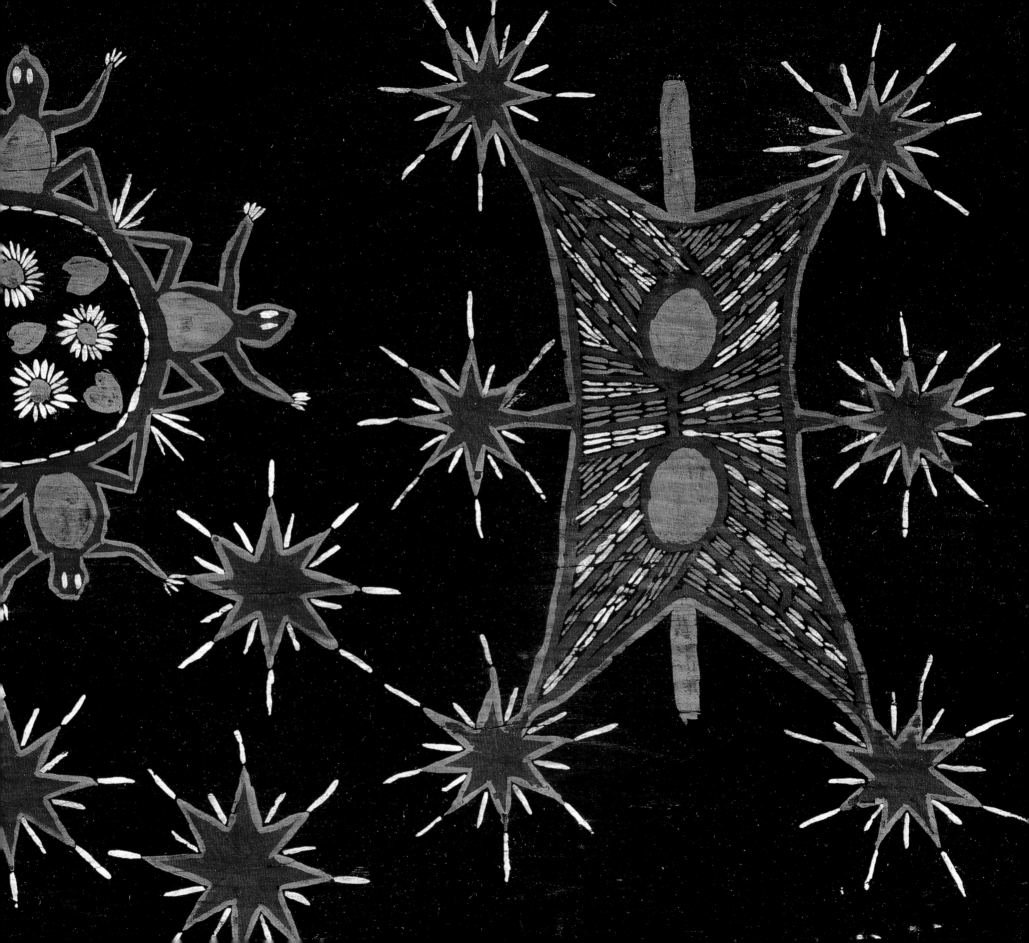

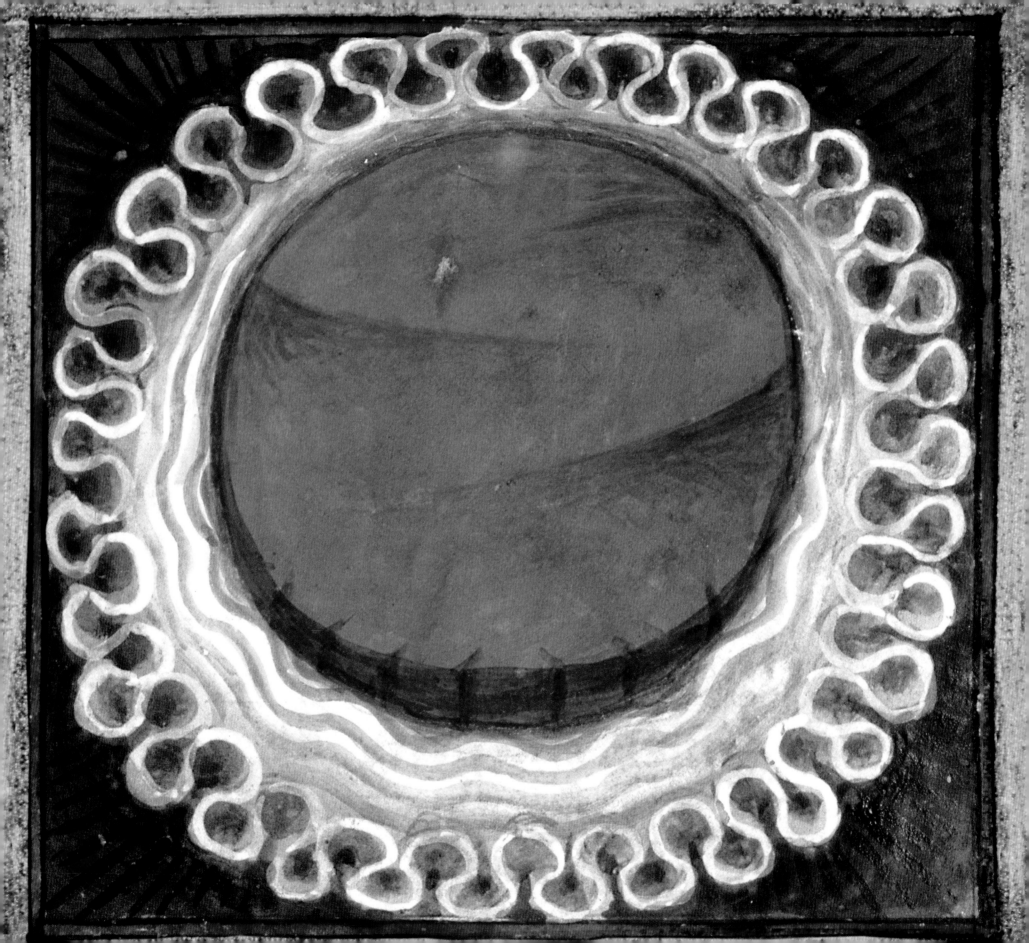

It does not matter that the ocean surrounds the Earth and that the exploration of countries is limited to those who can cross them; nor does it matter if the sky is a dome, a cover or the shell of a tortoise. A network of symbolic markers and reference signs that can be transmitted within the same social group as a common basis of identity, understanding and mutual recognition is essential to ensure one does not become lost in one's spatial environment, whether near or far.

The way in which the universe is portrayed represents a singular point of view that is just as logical as any other representation since it is created as a fable about the universe.

Once the story about the origins is finally created, a plausible explanation of natural phenomena is still required; a system of magical thinking is used that is legitimized, however, as a demonstrable or verifiable truth. In the absence of science, it becomes necessary to explain theoretically how the earth separated from the sky and why it remains suspended in space without falling. Is it thanks to the ocean that surrounds it and on which it floats like the yolk in an egg? This idea is seen in *On the Properties of Things* by Bartholomew the Englishman, a Franciscan monk who lived in the 13th century. The image appears in a 14th translation of the manuscript from Latin into French for Charles V, who would see in it a comprehensive survey of all that was known about the universe.

And the sea, is it a puddle or a bottomless abyss? And where is the kingdom of the dead? Is it in heaven or in hell? In the center of the Earth or below, in that unknown part bounded by a line on a map? Or are the stars souls, lighting the dark of the living? Is there a bridge to go from heaven to earth or a mountain that would allow access to the kingdom of the gods or the heavens? How does one know if the world is round or square or flat? Is the universe closed or infinite?

The Earth from On the Properties of Things,
by Bartholomew the Englishman. (1380–1395.
Sainte-Geneviève Library, Paris.)

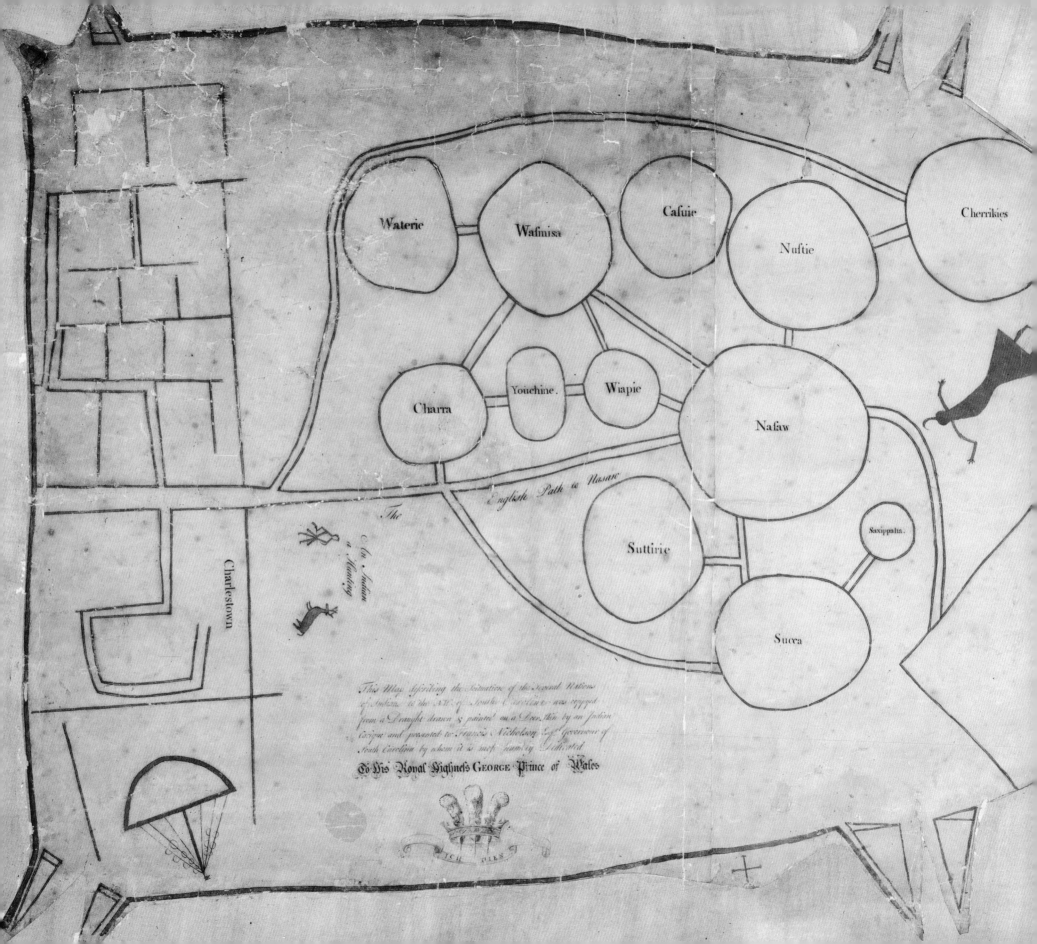

Wateric

Wafmisa

Cafuie

Nuftie

Cherrikies

Charra

Youchine.

Wiapie

Nafaw

Saxippaha.

English Path to Nafaw

The

An Indian a Hunting

Suttirie

Charlestown

Succa

This Map defcribing the Situation of the Several Nations
of Indians to the NW: of South Carolina, was coppyed
from a Draught drawn & painted on a Deer skin by an Indian
Cacique and prefented to Francis Nicholson Efq: Governour of
South Carolina by whom it is moft humbly Dedicated

To His Royal Highnefs GEORGE Prince of Wales

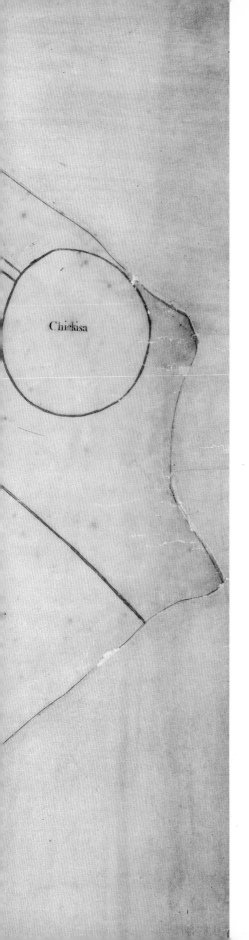

Chickisa

The questions people ask about the world never change from one culture to another. The answers, however, are many and unbelievably inventive, for everyone is invoked — the gods, spirits, ancestors, animals and demons — to understand the mystery of the Earth's origins. The representations are built through the myths, and the myths, in turn, lay the foundation for the people and the organization of their social, religious and value systems.

United States: Native American map on animal hide depicting the different tribes living in northeastern South Carolina.
(The British Library, London.)

Holy Places

In myths, the gods create or give birth to man. Humans — small clay statuettes baked in the sun like bricks that would sometimes have to be resculpted because they had been forgotten in the rain — resemble the universe: they carry inside them the imprint of divine omnipotence. There is no separation between nature and humans, small entities within a great one, but rather an interconnection: cosmos, city, house and body are caught in a matching game that can be found in holy, political and familial rituals. Everyone has their place in the universe, in their city and in their family. The one who governs and organizes the city is considered the representative of the gods on Earth. Any threat against the city is, therefore, a threat of disorder that is not only political but also cosmic; it is an attack on the gods who may seek revenge. The shaman, the sorcerer who heals the body, is also a priest and the holder of divine knowledge. He must, as such, restore the harmony that exists between the body and the universe, society and the divinities.

Therefore, the enemy lies on the side of the demons, those vanquished by the gods at the beginning of the world and those who, endlessly and everywhere, want the world to descend into chaos.

In this way, the holy stories about the origins link people together, but most importantly they weave an essential link and join the creator to the beings created, from the Earth to the heavens. The mythological understanding of the world is thus seen as sacred knowledge. It makes real that which cannot be seen or known.

In India, Brahman, the first person of the Hindu trinity, spends a year inside the cosmic egg then splits it in half to create the heavens and the earth and, between the two, the atmosphere, the eight cardinal points and the eternal home of the waters.

The Chinese version of the creation myth tells that from the primordial chaos in the great beginning — the immense emptiness — the world is born in China and is constantly being threatened with destruction by monsters and being saved by the benevolent divinities. The first giant, Pan Gu, sleeps inside the shell of the primordial egg. Too big, he breaks the egg and forms the heavens and the earth from the two halves, thus separating all that is light from all that is heavy. Then, tired of holding them at arm's length for 18,000 years, he sacrifices his body and his limbs before falling asleep so that they may form the universe.

A geocentric planetary system
representing the seventh day of creation,
from the Nuremberg Chronicle
by Hartmann Schedel.
(1493. Sainte-Geneviève Library, Paris.)

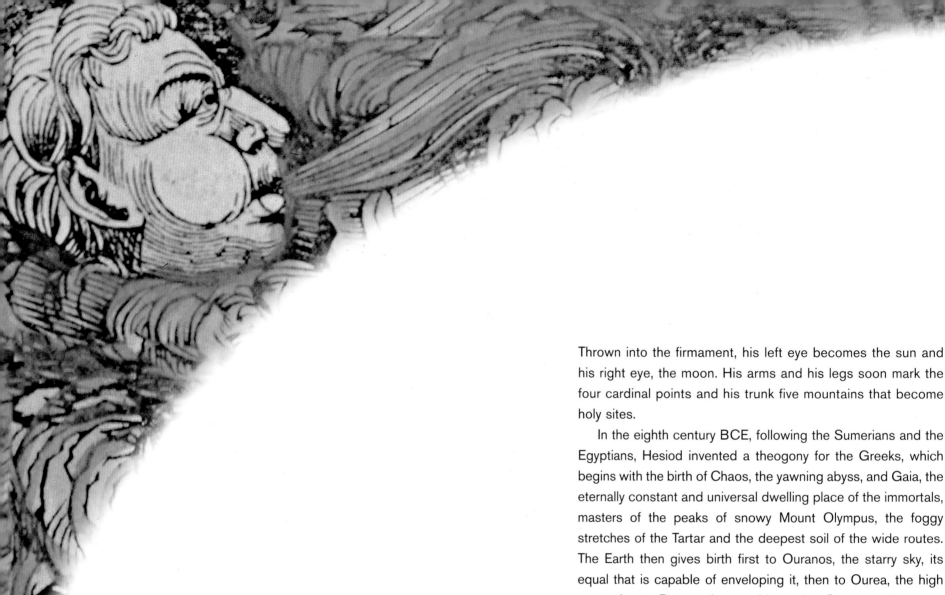

Thrown into the firmament, his left eye becomes the sun and his right eye, the moon. His arms and his legs soon mark the four cardinal points and his trunk five mountains that become holy sites.

In the eighth century BCE, following the Sumerians and the Egyptians, Hesiod invented a theogony for the Greeks, which begins with the birth of Chaos, the yawning abyss, and Gaia, the eternally constant and universal dwelling place of the immortals, masters of the peaks of snowy Mount Olympus, the foggy stretches of the Tartar and the deepest soil of the wide routes. The Earth then gives birth first to Ouranos, the starry sky, its equal that is capable of enveloping it, then to Ourea, the high mountains, to Pontos, the sea tide, and to Oceanos, the ocean river. Thus did the world come to be, according to Hesiod.

The stories contained in Genesis, the first book of the Bible, tell that, in the beginning, God created the heavens and the Earth. The Earth was empty and indistinct, and shadows covered the abyss. The breath of God swirled on the water, and God said, "Let there be light in this dark and indistinct world," and there was light. Then, God separated the light from the shadows. He also separated the waters, those under the firmament and those above it, so that, according to His word, the waters beneath the heavens gathered together and the continents appeared. God named it earth and sea, the mass of water from which earth arose. Thus the firmament, the starry sky visible to humans, became a space separating the two worlds, the one above and the one below, so that there was no confusion.

Many popular cosmogonies, legends and epics, regardless of the culture, tell of the creation of the sky, the earth and the seas. They often state that the sky and the earth were one before they were separated, and that everything was water before these beginnings. The deities then intervened in the course of natural events and the cycle of life. They appeared before the wise, the heroic and the saintly in specific places that, from then on, would be holy. The universe in which we live became a holy place because the divinities appeared in it. Temples were built on the exact locations of these theophanies, and the gods themselves are said to have dictated the architecture. Pillars were a certain way, supporting the world or, through their upward sweep, raising the prayers, sacrifices and offerings of people to the heavens. These temples were visible signs of possible communication with the gods. They would also be the place where, according as Mircea Eliade in *Myth and Reality,* the mystery of the origin and the revelation of creation were replayed. How could such a holy place not become the center of the universe?

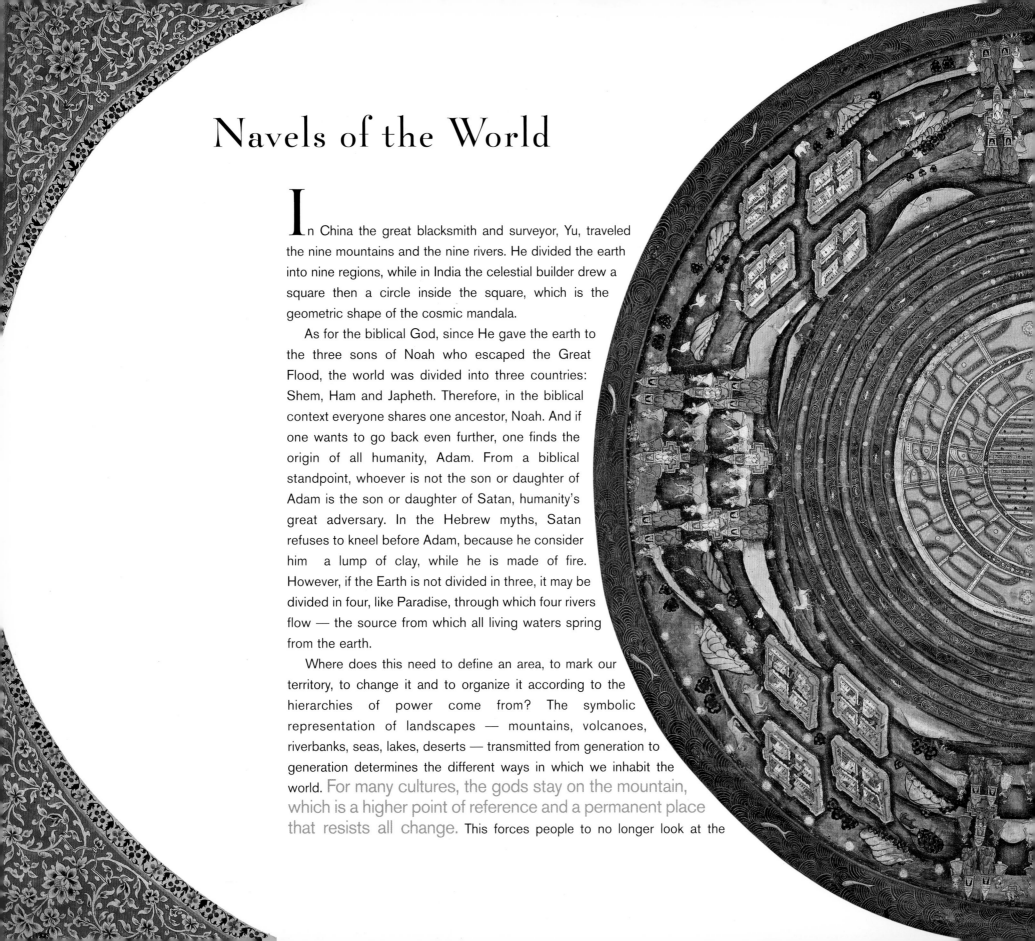

Navels of the World

In China the great blacksmith and surveyor, Yu, traveled the nine mountains and the nine rivers. He divided the earth into nine regions, while in India the celestial builder drew a square then a circle inside the square, which is the geometric shape of the cosmic mandala.

As for the biblical God, since He gave the earth to the three sons of Noah who escaped the Great Flood, the world was divided into three countries: Shem, Ham and Japheth. Therefore, in the biblical context everyone shares one ancestor, Noah. And if one wants to go back even further, one finds the origin of all humanity, Adam. From a biblical standpoint, whoever is not the son or daughter of Adam is the son or daughter of Satan, humanity's great adversary. In the Hebrew myths, Satan refuses to kneel before Adam, because he consider him a lump of clay, while he is made of fire. However, if the Earth is not divided in three, it may be divided in four, like Paradise, through which four rivers flow — the source from which all living waters spring from the earth.

Where does this need to define an area, to mark our territory, to change it and to organize it according to the hierarchies of power come from? The symbolic representation of landscapes — mountains, volcanoes, riverbanks, seas, lakes, deserts — transmitted from generation to generation determines the different ways in which we inhabit the world. For many cultures, the gods stay on the mountain, which is a higher point of reference and a permanent place that resists all change. This forces people to no longer look at the

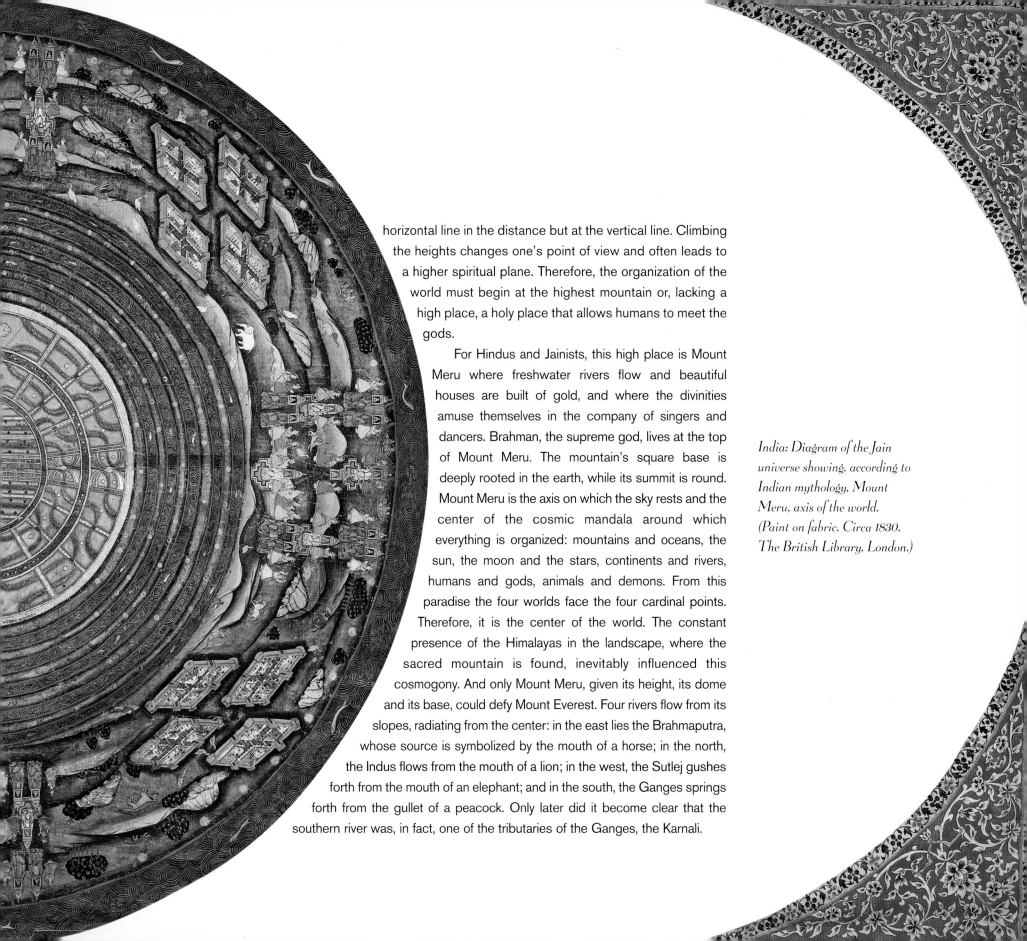

horizontal line in the distance but at the vertical line. Climbing the heights changes one's point of view and often leads to a higher spiritual plane. Therefore, the organization of the world must begin at the highest mountain or, lacking a high place, a holy place that allows humans to meet the gods.

For Hindus and Jainists, this high place is Mount Meru where freshwater rivers flow and beautiful houses are built of gold, and where the divinities amuse themselves in the company of singers and dancers. Brahman, the supreme god, lives at the top of Mount Meru. The mountain's square base is deeply rooted in the earth, while its summit is round. Mount Meru is the axis on which the sky rests and the center of the cosmic mandala around which everything is organized: mountains and oceans, the sun, the moon and the stars, continents and rivers, humans and gods, animals and demons. From this paradise the four worlds face the four cardinal points. Therefore, it is the center of the world. The constant presence of the Himalayas in the landscape, where the sacred mountain is found, inevitably influenced this cosmogony. And only Mount Meru, given its height, its dome and its base, could defy Mount Everest. Four rivers flow from its slopes, radiating from the center: in the east lies the Brahmaputra, whose source is symbolized by the mouth of a horse; in the north, the Indus flows from the mouth of a lion; in the west, the Sutlej gushes forth from the mouth of an elephant; and in the south, the Ganges springs forth from the gullet of a peacock. Only later did it become clear that the southern river was, in fact, one of the tributaries of the Ganges, the Karnali.

India: Diagram of the Jain universe showing, according to Indian mythology, Mount Meru, axis of the world. (Paint on fabric. Circa 1830. The British Library, London.)

Turkey. God created the Earth,
the planets and the stars
in the sky. First page of
the Book of Creation
(Sefer Yetzirah). 15th century
Armenian manuscript. Istanbul.
University library.

Whether the landscapes described are real or imaginary, they help organize religious, political and familial spaces. The different perceptions of the body also contribute to a representation of the universe and vice versa. The navel — a central point and vital mark — is replaced by a navel of the world inscribed in the matrix of the universe, a point where the divinity appears and where the circle also symbolizes the sky. The routes drawn from the center are like so many ropes that secure people to the gods, wherever they may be. The pilgrimage routes are what bring people back to their own fulfillment — the much-desired meeting with the divine.

Different religions each fashion an original story in their sacred texts about the world where humans can find themselves face-to-face with God, and they place the basis of their faith at its center. It is a center that is both cosmic and mystical to which people must turn for their salvation. They must also sometimes travel in order to embrace the entirety of the created universe, divine revelation and the imperfect human condition.

In the representation of Genesis introducing the first book of the Creation in an Armenian manuscript, the world reads like a spiritual route. Adam and Eve appear in the first circle under the irreverent moon, which sticks out its tongue and spins around in spite of us, like the months of the year. Paradise, an inaccessible land, and the tree of life are located at the top of this map of the universe that is divided into three, while a whole series of monsters, unaware of the existence of the true God, are relegated to the bottom and surrounded by distinct black and red boxes, the colors of shadows and hell.

God revealed himself in Jerusalem, its holy area protected by a circle, a recognizable and impenetrable boundary between the sacred and the profane. However, He is positioned above the lunar world and its cycle, and He remains outside the circle of the universe and its planetary organization, demonstrating that the Creator cannot be confused with his creation. The angels shower him with praise. As for the stole covering his shoulders, it evokes the sacerdotal garments of the head of the Armenian apostolic church. Thus, Jerusalem, divine authority and religious legitimacy overlap as part of the same understanding of the center of the world.

In his biography of the prophet Mohammed, Martin Lings states, "[Beginning with Abraham], there were two spiritual currents, two religions, two worlds devoted to God; two circles and, as a result, two centres. A place is never holy because man chooses it to be so, but because it was chosen in heaven." The Valley of Bacca (which became, much later, Makka, or Mecca) is where Hagar, Abraham's second wife, and his son Ishmael stayed in the desert. Far from the caravan route, lost and thirsty, Hagar feared her child would die. She climbed two nearby mountains, passing seven times between them to see if help was coming. In her distress, she beseeched God, and God heard her. He caused a river to spring from the desert sand. Soon, the caravans stopped at the miracle well, the well of Zamzam. This well became a place of spiritual healing. God showed Abraham, who had come to visit Ishmael, the exact spot where he should build a sanctuary with his son, and He teaches them how to construct it. Called the Kaaba (which means "cube"), it will be a cubic sanctuary. Its four points shall face the four cardinal points. Stone whiter than milk brought from Paradise by an angel, which the sins of Adam's sons have blackened, would be embedded in the eastern part of the Kabaa. This is how God's sanctuary, the holy House, became the center of the world.

All cultures have chosen and laid out the spaces designated as the center of the universe. Rome and the holy wall that surrounds it; Delphi and its omphalos hidden under the temple of Apollo; Easter Island where a round stone, Te Pito Kura, focuses cosmic energy; Cuzco, capital of the Incas. Churches, mosques, temples, sanctuaries and dressed stones are all reference points that are part of the landscape, direct the gaze and build networks of routes that help spread or expand the sacred truth. They are signs, and they are inscribed on maps to guide the faithful.

Emperors' palaces or kings' castles would also be built to become centers of command and convergence. Versailles, seat of Louis the 14th of France, the Sun King, was designed with rectilinear avenues radiating from around the château to distribute the royal energy throughout the kingdom and to cause the tributes of the people to converge toward political power. The same was done in Rome and Beijing, as though the symbolic and the pragmatic go hand in hand. Thus, humans imagined the center of all centers, the earth of humans, to be the center of the universe.

Plan of Mecca: Map showing Mediterranean ports by Ali Ahmad ibn Muhammad al-Sharqî. (National Library of France, Paris.)

From One Point to Another

"The Kazvin route. First, it follows the valley of the willows. The mountains are round and very near, the river is noisy and the fords terrible. Then, the valley widens to become a broad swampy plateau still covered with patches of snow. The river is lost in the distance, one's gaze too."

Nicolas Bouvier, *The Way of the World.*

Drawing a route requires changing the landscape, even if the route simply runs from one point to another and is nothing more than a serpent made of earth, slithering across the grass, the forests and mountains. The route must be repeated so that the imprint left by feet and horses' hooves clears a path. The purpose of traveling from one point to another must be necessary, vital or important if others are, in turn, to follow the same route. Those who return from whence they came will have already tried the route. They will have memorized the landscape and their surroundings based on all that is noticeable: escarpments, rivers, majestic trees. They will have created in their minds an image of the place by visualizing it and by connecting different reference points. If they want to communicate this route to others, they will, no doubt, point out everything that lines the route and confirms that they are on the right path. They may even draw the crossings, the dangers and the fords on the ground.

Over the centuries, Native Americans memorized their routes by singing: "The world had been created by the Ancestors who, once they had come out of the earth, began their travels. While walking, they sang, naming things so that they would exist." Their song described the features of the landscape they were creating. Each nomadic Native American is the beneficiary of his or her mythical Ancestor and this is why, if they own no land, the route they sing about belongs to them.

In traditional societies, of what use would maps have been when words and memories were always needed to build history? That which was known was transmitted from memory to memory. It was the same for the topography of the land — wells, pastures, places to hunt, to trade and to welcome. If visual support became necessary, it could only be transitory and for immediate use. Drawings, considered the equivalent of maps, were mostly of sacred and magical value and used for incantations to the gods and for protection. These "maps" also described the travels of the shaman or the sorcerer in search of a soul devoured by the spirits and its route in the underworld. Using symbols, they indicated the pitfalls encountered along the way.

It is our observation of nature — a subject of science or contemplation, domination or harmony — that guides the way we represent the landscape. For the Chinese, the space is crossed by a vital path that cuts across the earth like breath through the human body, according to "life lines" on the ground that converge at the point where they stop. For the Chinese, painting, as François Jullien highlights in *The Propensity of*

Things, is like trying to find a trace of the cosmic pulse through the paintbrush, a portrayal of the landscape as it appears in nature. The mountains and the rivers obey this intuition. And, by standing back a little and placing some distance between this play of lines and oneself, one can see them as they alternate and contrast, rise or stop.

The word "paint" in Chinese, according to a very old etymology, means "outline by drawing." But the painter is not a cartographer, and when drawing an outline, when he is called upon to sketch his travels, he can take some liberty with the reality of each place. He will, no doubt, emphasize the difficulties of the landscape, such as the dangerous passes overcome by the expedition. But it would be very difficult to redo the voyage. The maps of the travels of Vietnamese officials in China were prepared with this idea in mind. The painter showed how elevation, relief and slope demanded perseverance in order to reach China. The differently colored routes crisscross, but might one be a stream? Do they go around a village or indicate a stop, or, do the colors indicate a trip there and back?

沿甕山茁屬
江漢社一
册使至此例
待中秋

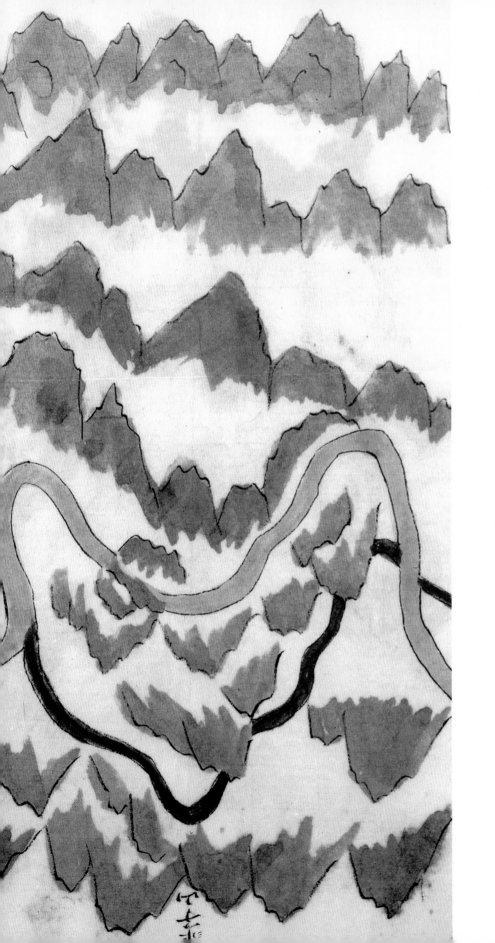

Vietnam: Collection of maps of the travels of Vietnamese officials in China. (18th century. Collège de France, Asian Society, Paris.)

According to the experts, long before the Spanish conquest of Mexico by Hernan Cortes in 1519, the palaces of Moctezuma, the emperor of Mexico, contained libraries filled with theological, astrological and geographical manuscripts. The emperor possessed maps of his domain of different sizes and shapes: round, square and rectangular. They accurately noted marked linear routes and also recorded where tragic or triumphant historical events took place. Each color on the map corresponded to a cardinal point and provided an idea of where the place was found. The colors could also be symbolic; for example a red lake indicated that there had been a massacre at that location. As for the drawings of the routes themselves, they were covered by the traces of bare feet that had traveled from one point to another. The map was a way of finding one's way and an instrument to tell the history of the Aztecs. Their maps were systematically destroyed by the Spanish, as were many other signs of idolatry, because they did not obviously meet European cartographic criteria.

Mexico: Lienzo de Tetlama, a nahuatl manuscript. (Early 19th century. National Library of France Paris.)

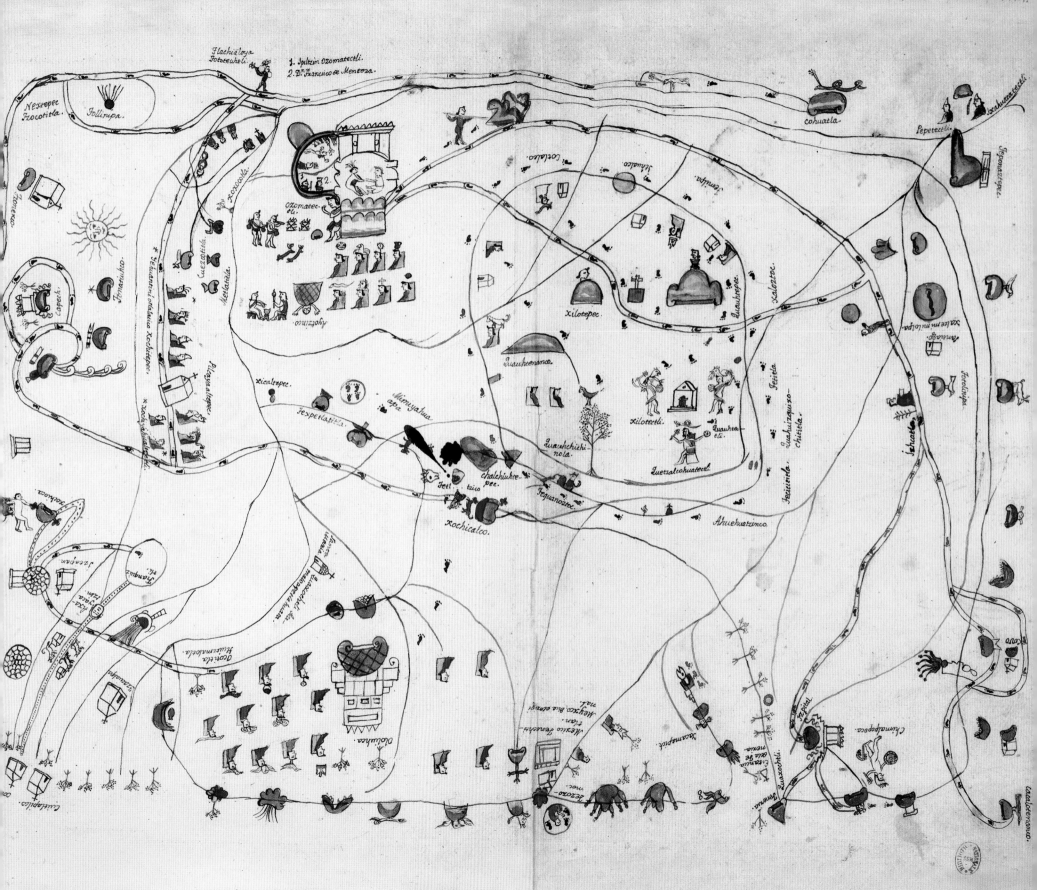

Septentrionalium Terrarum descriptio. Per Gerardum Mercatorem Cum Privilegio.

Frisl: lant insula.

Farre in: sulę. Nordero. Sudero. Farre. Dumo. Bishops sound. Diamanten sound. Diamanten scopuli.

Scctland insulæ. Fairé fl id est pulchra insula.

SEP: TENTRIO: NALIVM Terrarum de: scriptio. Per Gerardum Mercatorem Cum Privilegio.

Spheres and Poles

I f the Earth were round — as the geographers Hecatee of Milet (6th century BCE) and Eratosthenes (circa 276–194 BCE), who knew how to make globes and indicated information gathered by travelers, claimed based on their calculations — the world known to the Greeks represented, in reality, only a small part of the globe.

Following the Greco-Roman legacy and the influence of the theories of Aristotle (384–322 BCE), rediscovered during the Middle Ages in the West, the world was shown as a circle of four elements assembled in the form of a sphere that, by the wonders of the heavens, surround the Earth, which is stuck in the middle. Such was the popular theory during the 14th century, recalled in "The World in General," the first chapter in Book VIII of Bartholomew the Englishman's *On the Properties of Things.* But the figure of the circle, like that of the center, also becomes a decorative pattern that is reproduced in the margins of maps, like the plate of the northern hemisphere seen from above on the opposite page.

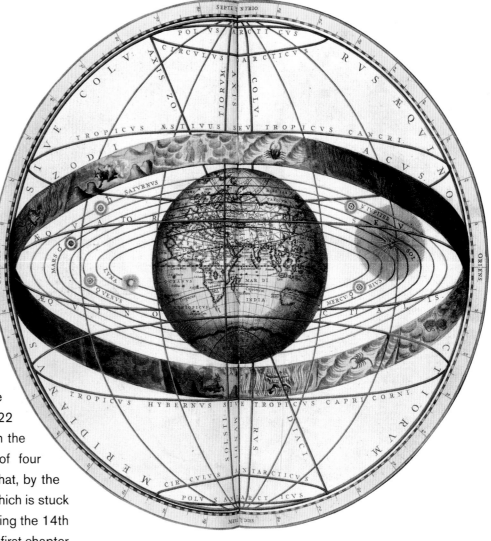

PAGE OPPOSITE: *Europe: View of the northern hemisphere drawn by Gerard Mercator from* Atlas, or Cosmographic Meditations on the Fabric of the World and the Figure of the Fabrick'd. *(1595. The British Library, London.)*

ABOVE: *Globe of the Earth in the Ptolemy's solar system and surrounded by the constellations and the signs of the Zodiac. (The British Library, London.)*

B ut where are the limits of the Earth? What is at the top of the world? Is it an ocean or a continent? Pythagoras (circa 570–480 BCE) and Plato (427–348 BCE) explained that a world opposite to the known world must exist so the latter does not fall of balance. They called this "opposite" Earth Antichthon. It is inhabited by people who walk with their feet in the air, called the Antipodes. In this country where the beings are so strange it is very hot, the seas are boiling and the monsters that guard access to this land are fierce. This theory solved the problem of the spherical Earth populated by humans everywhere.

When *Geography* by Ptolemy (90–168 CE), who prepared maps of the sky and the earth, was printed in 1475, no one knew what really happens at the poles. Since the constellation Ursa dominated the northern regions, the Greeks referred to these lands as Arkos ("bear" in Greek), which led to the Arctic. They invented the word Antarctica for the lands opposite.

In 1497 Portuguese navigators, who had little time for philosophy, were opening a route into the southern hemisphere. They must have thought the illustrious Ptolemy had passed on to them a lot of good information about the geography, but that he was wrong about one point. As they passed through the tropics, they found no boiling seas or monsters, but they did find vegetation and lots of people. In addition, when all the passages to China closed because of conflicts relating to the Arab conquest, travelers headed to the northeast to find a route, something the whales had been doing for thousands of years. How could Ptolemy have imagined these lands at the end of the earth, far from the known and inhabited world, except as something frightening and akin the kingdom of death?

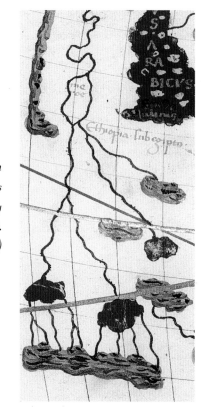

Florence: Map of the world in conical projection by Nicolaus Germanus, from Cosmography *by Ptolemy. (Circa 1460–1470. National Library of France, Paris.)*

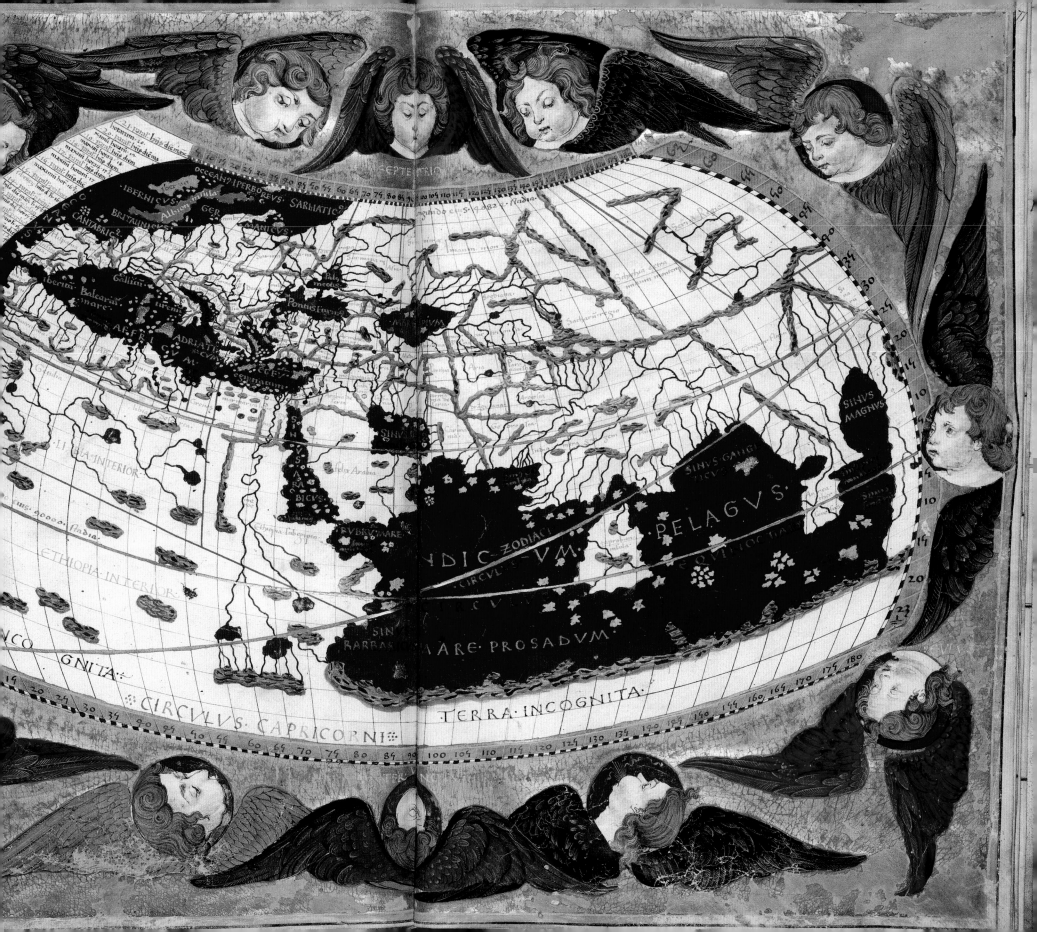

LEFT: *Picture of a sea serpent, detail from a map by Urbano Monte. (16th century. The British Library, London.)*

OPPOSITE PAGE: *Jerusalem is shown in the center of the universe and surrounded by three continents (Europe, Asia and Africa). The principal Christian religious centers are indicated, including Rome. (National Library of France, Paris.)*

AMERICA
Die Newe
Welt.

Engeland

Franckreich

Saxen

Lothringen Deudschland

Behemen Reussen

Polen

EVROPA Vngern Moschaw

Belschland Türckey

Griechen-
land

Roma 382.

ARMENIA MEDEN

Ninue 171. Rages 349.

MESOPO-
TAMIA ASIA PER-
SIA INDIA

SYRIA Haran 110. Persepolis

Antiochia 70. CHALDEA Susa 230.

Damascu 40. Babylon 170.

Vr 156.

ARABIA

Saba 312.

IERVSALEM

Das grosse Mittelmeer Das Rote Meer.

der Arch.

Alexandria 72.

Egypten

Cyrene 204.

LYBIA Meroe 24.

Morenland

AFRICA

Köngreich
Melinde.

CAPVT BO-
næ spei.

SE LIVRE FVT ACHEVE
Par guillaume Le Testu Le cinq iesme
Jour dapuril 1555 Auant pasques

"Is the Earth elongated or flat at the poles? This is the famous question long debated by scientists. The ingenious systems imagined here and there, and the geometric and astronomical operations performed until 1735 were not enough to answer the question." Thus begins the journal by the reverend Outhier, who was a member of the expedition led by Maupertuis in Laponia in 1736. This expedition was ordered by Louis XV and the Academy of Sciences to verify the shape of the Earth. La Condamine and other scientists went to Peru and the equator to take measurements. A comparison of their results would decide whether or not the Earth is the shape of a perfect sphere or, as Maupertuis insisted, a mandarin orange! Were the Greek philosophers wrong to claim that the Earth is round? It was necessary to know the true length of the degrees of the meridian in the north or the parallel circles in the south so that navigators would no longer be exposed to the dangers resulting from errors.

Globes, like atlases, reflected the image of what was known. As the image moved away from the familiar world, it would become more and more inexact. To fill the gap left by all that remained unknown, what could be better than to invent? Maps must maintain their function: to show the size of the world and the extent of what was known, but they also needed to show the extent of an area's political power. Globes also bear witness to geographical and astronomical knowledge. Certainly, they increased the need for conquest by offering new places that one would swear are uninhabited all the way to the royal houses.

The Earth at the center of the nine spheres of the universe, of which it is the fixed pivot; the Earth of man, divided in three, in four, lengthwise, widthwise, drawn with south or north at the top; fertile or arid earth where trade routes are created; the earth where the flow of rivers traces the navigable waterways, where the mountains calling to meet with the gods trace the pilgrimage routes… All these images owe their existence to our need to know what lies beyond the horizon, the need that makes us always advance on firm footing, on the dust of the earth.

North Pole. Map according to a star projection where four zones represent the surface of the Earth, from Cosmographie Universelle *(Universal cosmography) drawn by the French cartographer and explorer Guillaume Le Testu. The title box indicates that this book was printed in 1555, on the fifth day of April, before Easter. (Ministry of Defense, Defense Historical Services, Paris.)*

Geographers in the Field

Finding One's Bearings

*"Travelling seems to me to be a profitable exercise.
The soul is continuously stimulated by noticing
new and unknown things."*

Montaigne, Essays

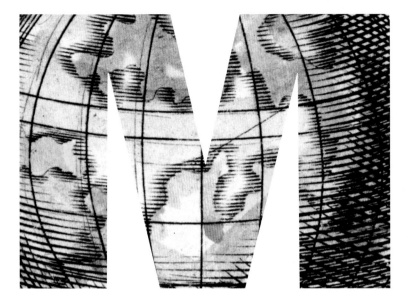

apmaking may be one of the oldest arts. People have used all kinds of media to design them. Native Americans drew vast territories of rivers and lakes on tree bark and on the flat bones of animals. The Micronesians of the Marshall Islands invented maps to navigate long waterways using a few palm leaves and shells. The Inuit carved in wood.

The oldest map that we possess is Babylonian and is not based on any real measurement of the Earth, but it does introduce a geometric representation by mapping small parcels of land and defining their surface area. In Egypt, this same grid system helped to draw and redraw the boundaries of fertile land regularly flooded by the Nile. Therefore, a basic knowledge of surveying was essential and with it, the invention of measurement. Inaccurate and sometimes fanciful, maps were still useful. How can one govern an empire, travel or achieve military objectives without any markers? There was no other solution but to leave it to others to calculate the dimensions of the earth.

In 2nd century Greece, Eratosthenes carried out the first measurements. He determined that the circumference of the earth was the equivalent of 24,662 miles (39,690 km), a figure that was very close to reality. His method? Linking geography to geometry and astronomy. His map showed the three continents then known, Europe, Libya (Africa) and Asia, as reproduced by travelers in their accounts and drawings. In 160 CE, Ptolemy, an astronomer and geographer, created a large map of the world that was the source of all future cartographic works. Using astronomy, he determined 350 fixed points and indicated 8,000 places. His maps, preserved by the Arabs, remained undiscovered in Europe until the Renaissance.

In the 13th and 14th centuries, the use of a compass became more widespread, which led to the creation of portolan nautical charts. It was a revolution not only in the field of mapmaking, but also in the creation of the tools needed to read maps. Drawn on hides, portolans provided a detailed description of the ports and the coasts but rarely the interior of the land. Graphometers, stymographs, map loupes and other instruments, often produced using precious materials, began to appear.

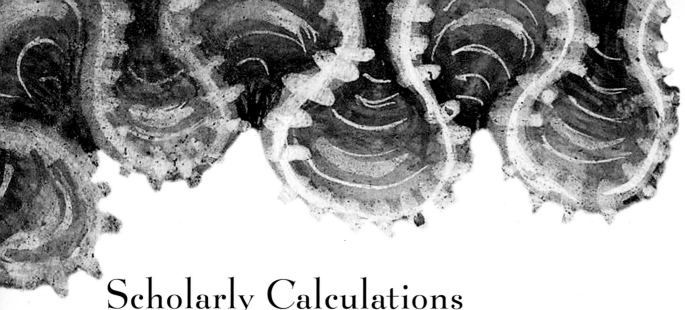

Scholarly Calculations

There was a time in Greece when the poets and the myths they sang about no longer sufficed to explain the world. Without a doubt, a decisive turning point came in the 7th century BCE, when writing was no longer reserved for the privileged caste, but a tool that could be used to reveal knowledge to the masses. For the early philosophers, it would be a way to form rational thinking. The procreation of Gaia and the authority of Zeus were then relegated to the level of useless, even dangerous, fables. To study nature, its changes and its future, to seek the principle that governs the universe, to see how each element of the world is part of a larger whole and to give meaning to this arrangement was, from that moment on, the watchwords of reason.

Pythagoras developed a theory and calculations to prove that the Earth is a sphere. Some 20 centuries later, Denis Guedj enthused in *The Measure of the World* that this theory should be loudly proclaimed and commented that "that the Earth is round is unexpected good luck." And yet, as Maupertuis would prove several centuries after Pythagoras by using triangulation, it was not quite perfectly round. Maupertuis demonstrated that for one who wants to determine the size of a solid, the sphere has two advantages: one piece of data, the radius or circumference, suffices to define it, and this measurement can be taken anywhere because a sphere's radius of curvature is constant.

Moreover, Maupertuis showed that the earth has a preferred axis, the poles. He also showed that, among all the great, equivalent circles of the sphere, there are preferred ones that go through the poles, which are the meridians. Each point on the globe can be found on a meridian, which can be determined by moving from north to south. The measurement of the meridians made it possible to know the size of the Earth. Geodesy, the part of geometry that consists of dividing any shape into a certain number of sections, arrived in time to support geometry.

God depicted as the Great Architect of the Universe draws the outline of the earth with his compass and delineates three places, which He gives to the three sons of Noah. Bible historiale *belonging to Petrus Comestor. Mazarine Library, Paris.*

When Plato founded the Academy in 387 BCE, the most rigorous knowledge was taught: astronomy, geometry and arithmetic. He took care to have carved on the facade of the Academy "That no one enter here who is not a surveyor." One of his contemporaries, the astronomer Eudox of Knidos (304–355 BCE), was also excited by spheres, and he would describe 27 of them to explain the motions of the world!

A little later, Aristotle embarked on a study of the cosmos and divided it into two distinct regions: the earth and the heavens. Aristotle theorized that the moon serves as a frontier and that above it the world of the stars moves in perfect circles within their own spheres. Below is our world, with its various motions: increase, decrease, generation and corruption. Everything is in its place, and the world is organized. Reason reigns over the earth as in the heavens. The harmony and the beauty of the proportions — that is the secret of the universe.

OPPOSITE PAGE: *The* Bréviaire d'amour *(Breviary of love) by Matfre Ermengau depicts angels using a crank. (13th century. National Library of France, Paris.).*

ABOVE: *A surveyor measures a piece of land using a map and a compass in* Traité d'arpentage *(Acreage treaty) by Arnaud de Villeneuve. (15th century. Inguimbertine Library, Carpentras.)*

It is not surprising then that numbers and reasoning quickly found their place in the notion that humans are made of the earthly surface. Geodesy involved the measuring fields and dividing land into a grid, thereby imposing on nature a geometry that organized and defined civilized areas in relation to wild ones. The Greeks structured space according to their rational concept of the world and the gods, who they believed were the great organizers of the cosmos with its immutable laws. The temples were built up high and dominated the landscape, crops were distributed in a grid pattern and cities were laid out along right-angled streets.

It is said that the Greeks learned about the straight line, the circle, the ruler and the compass from Egyptian surveyors. They never suspected that by holding a rope between two points they would help others imagine measurements other than those used to chart the fertile fields of the Nile, which eats away a little of the surface area during each of its floods.

ABOVE: *Title box from the manuscript of the map of the Pyrenees by Lhuillier and Villaret. (1719. Reproduced with the kind permission of the National Geographic Institute, Paris.)*

OPPOSITE PAGE: *According to the Greek model, the structure of the world corresponds to a mathematical model. In this image, the ruler, the compass and the square represent the tools of knowledge.* (1634. Novissima ac exactissima totius orbis terrarum descriptio [The newest and most exact description of the lands of the whole globe], *Jocodus II Hondius, cartographer, and Henricus Hondius, publisher. National Library of France, Paris.)*

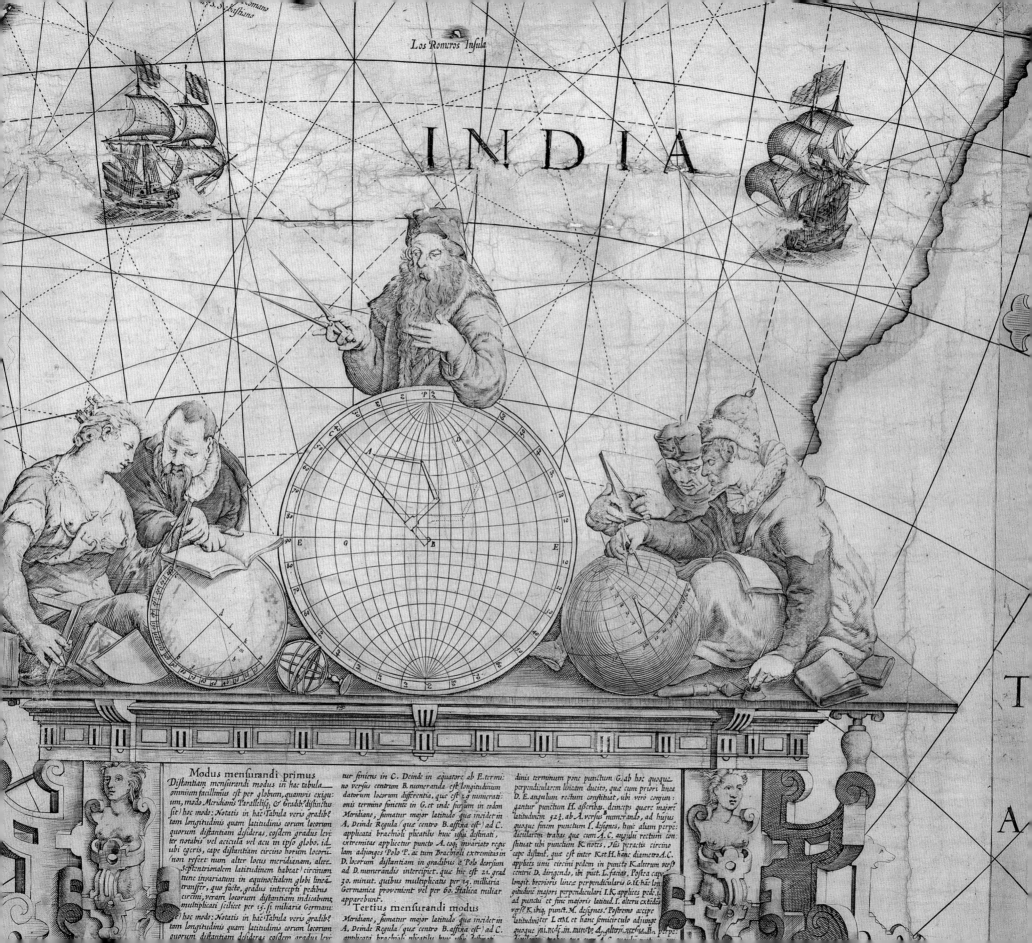

To measure, organize and find: is the world so dangerous that attempts have to be made to control it and make it fit inside limits? What do we fear by venturing away from the gods and beyond the familiar horizon — without resorting to warlike imperialism and without being equipped with our mental structures — to grasp the unknown? The fear is, no doubt, to be out of one's depth. But can the reason that makes the world intelligible and arranges our perceptions in the right order alone make the world accessible to us? What do we do with the emotion caused by the beauty of the landscape and our intimacy with the spirit of a place?

In order to make their world intelligible, philosophers needed input from those who surveyed the land, literally and figuratively. Their astonishment and their reflections were also fed by the observations and practical knowledge brought back to the administrators of cities and empires. What is the topography of a landscape? The distance from one point of water to another or from one city to the sea or a river? And the climate, is it dry or humid? And what about the fauna and flora? But all of these "territorializations" of space, which we describe as a country (chorography) or a piece of land (topography), also allow for baselines.

False title page of the Gran et nouveau atlas de la marine hydrographique dans lequel est compris & desmonstré toutes les côtes du monde connu *(Big and new atlas of marine hydrography in which all the coasts of the known world are included and shown) by Johannes Van Keulen. (1715. Volume 2. Part 1, published in Amsterdam. Municipal Library, Versailles.)*

According to Gilles Deleuze, these baselines make it possible to create something else. These baselines that intertwine may be expertly drawn from one point to another, but what do they say about this world that they divide into triangles and parts of circles? While they seem boring to those who do not have a geometric mind and get lost trying to understand the measurements, by pushing on the space of maps, they may help others to leave the plowed furrow and allow their imagination to rise up.

Thus, despite its reported estimations and its perfected instruments designed to determine one's location and destination, geography would remain an invitation to travel combined with a certain philosophy of life. Leaving home to discover other lands means accepting to meet the unknown face to face and asking oneself "Who am I?" Unless, of course, one is in such a hurry to invade the so-called virgin territories of other cultures that one does not pay attention to the representations that lie outside the circle of reason. A good use of geography may have been made by Socrates (470–399 BCE), who cut down the pride of the sophist Alcibiades by showing him a map of the world. He explained to him that the domains of which he was so proud occupied no more space on the map than a simple dot.

Every Which Way

For those who seek definitions, the encyclopedia by Diderot and d'Alembert, originally published between 1751 and 1780, is a true delight. The article on "Geographer" states that the term is said of someone versed in geography and, in particular, of those who have contributed to the advancement of this science through their works. The authors explain that those who publish maps in which there is nothing new and who only copy — sometimes poorly — the work of others, do not deserve to be called geographers, as they are nothing more than publishers.

It appears that during the century of the Enlightenment not just anyone could call themselves a geographer! However, there were apparently many imposters. Not only were they not geographers, but their maps were wrong, as they continued to print maps that should have been corrected following new expeditions. However, engraving new maps was expensive, especially if the publisher had not yet depleted his stock of old maps.

Travelers did indeed encounter problems because of outdated and incorrect maps. "I also had the opportunity to notice that the Salvages are in the wrong place on Mr. Bellin's map," remarked Louis Antoine de Bougainville as he began his voyage to the Rio de la Plata near Buenos Aires in 1766. "Moreover, on the 18th [of November] we spotted Palm Island to the corrected southwest by west, and, according to Mr. Bellin, it should have been to the southwest. I was able to conclude from these two observations that Mr. Bellin located Salvages Island thirty-two minutes further west than it actually was. As for Dr. Halley's English map, Salvages Island lies another thirty leagues west of Mr. Bellin's." Was Bougainville annoyed to see all these mistakes on his nautical chart? Or was he happy to be able to correct them, thus revealing the ignorance of those who had not made the trip?

Geography certainly needs artist-geographers and printers, but it needs navigators even more. The famous Jacques Nicolas Bellin (1703–1772) began working at the Depository of Maps and Drawings of the Navy in France when it was founded in 1721. He worked there for 50 years. Bougainville had taken the heavy volumes of *Le Neptune français* (*The French Neptune*) with him on board *La Boudeuse* to help him navigate during his voyage in 1766, but they dated from 1693! Bellin had republished the work in 1753, but in its original version. He had engraved on copper plates, which still exist, that the volume consisted of a frame prepared by Maraldi (1665–1729) and Cassini de Thury (1625–1712) that is graduated according to longitude and latitude and is supposed to conform to the grid system of the map of France. In reality, it was a practical but artificial veneer on a completely outdated background, Alain Morgat explained in detail during a conference on *Le Neptune français* in 2002.

Bellin is a cartographer who sits in his study and compiles and analyzes the maps brought back by boat captains. The armchair travels he drew with enthusiasm found their limits when tested by the seas.

England: Theatre of the World *by Abraham Ortelius. (1605. Engraving on copper. Sotheby's, London.)*

The petty scholarly disputes between geographers contributed to perpetuating incorrect locations, but they also helped to advance knowledge. Sometimes mapmakers considered the information provided by their competition impossible, and some simply preferred to continue in error rather than admit the truth if it was shown by a rival.

Eratosthenes (circa 276–194 BCE) garnered many prestigious titles — among them, mathematician, cartographer and director of the Great Library at Alexandria. He fraternized with scholars and philosophers from around the world. It is to him, with his calculations and methods, that we owe the word "geography." Eratosthenes — whose reputation, as stated in Diderot and d'Alembert's encyclopedia, matched the extent of his genius — fought the geographic inaccuracies of his age and devoted three books to his geographical comments. He wanted to denounce faulty knowledge and correct the ancient map of Anaximander (610–546 BCE), a disciple of Thales of Milet (circa 625–547 BCE), who was the first to reproduce the Earth on a globe. Eratosthenes communicated his observations in a third treaty, but there were also errors in his maps, and new corrections were added to it.

It is said that Pytheas the Massaliote, a geographer under Alexander in the 4th century BCE, was so passionate about geography that he could not confine himself to only observing his own country. He traveled around Europe, from the columns of Hercules to the mouth of the Tanais, and he crossed the ocean to the Arctic Circle, where he noted that the farther north he traveled, the longer the days became. Pytheas designated these differences in days as "climates." Centuries later, he, too, was cast in doubt and accused of lying by the Greek Strabo (circa 58 BCE–25 CE), during the reign of Octavius Augustus. Greece had by that time become part of Rome, and Strabo wanted to add his knowledge to that of other geographers and give the Roman Empire the information it needed to govern better. He could not stop himself from treating Pytheas, with his trip north, as a liar. He said that no one could go to uninhabited countries; otherwise, why would the Roman legions not have tried to colonize them? Nevertheless, Pytheas had certainly reached Iceland.

Iceland. Theatre of the World by Abraham Ortelius (1606. The British Library, London.)

ISLANDIA.

Septentrio

BLOE.

WESTFIORDVNG.

NORDLEN
DINGAFIOR
DVNG.

Sand
Iokul.

Arnafelds Iokul.

Getlands Iokul.

Bald Iokul.

Skialbred.

SVNDLEN
DINGAFIOR
DVNG.

Hekla

SKALHOLT sedes
episcopalis, cui
adiuncta est schola.

AVSTLENDIN
GAFIORDVNG

Medalland.

Oriens

AVLLOS.

Meridies

ILLVSTRISS. AC POTENTISS.
REGI FREDERICO II DANIAE,
NORVEGIAE, SLAVORVM, GO
THORVMQVE REGI, ETC. PRIN
CIPI SVO CLEMENTISSIMO,
ANDREAS VELLEIVS
DESCRIBEB. ET DEDICABAT.

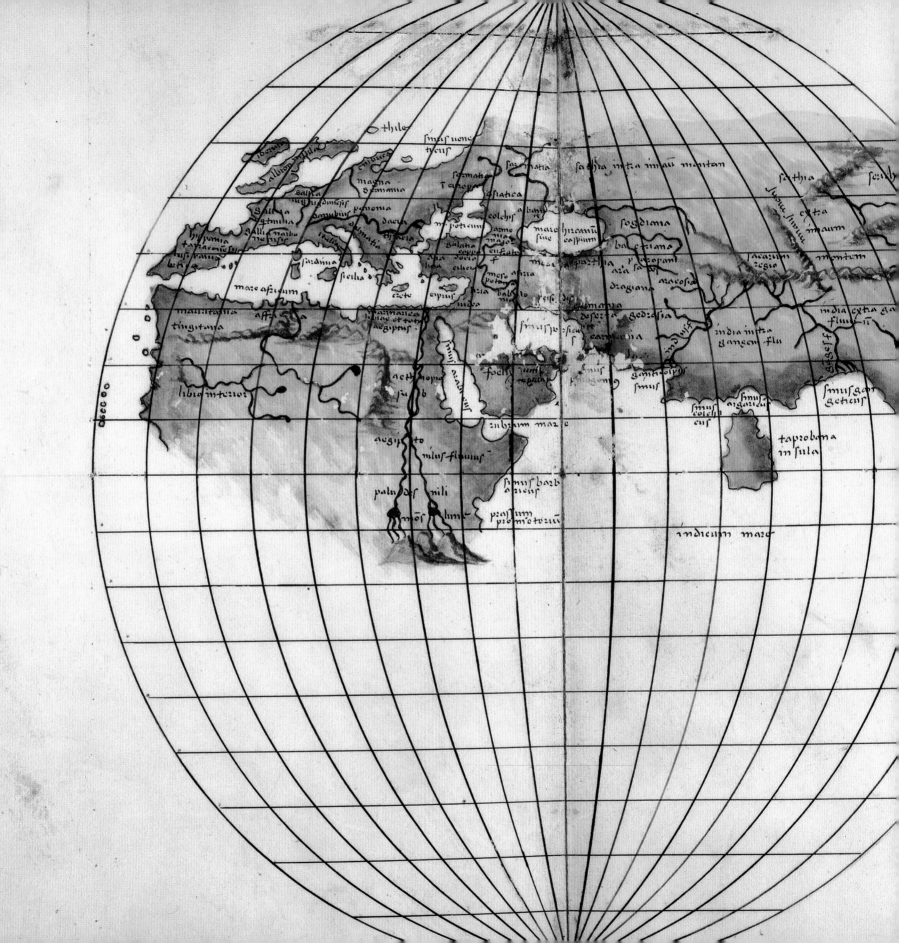

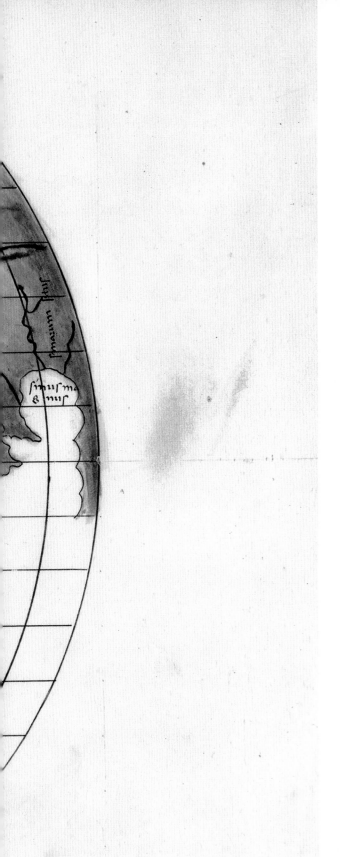

Confident his knowledge was legitimate, Strabo denounced the bad faith of Hipparchus of Nicea (165–127 BCE), a Greek astronomer whose character was as frightening as his criticisms. It is said Hipparchus detested Eratosthenes's corrections and preferred to choose what he believed to be the lesser of two evils: he reassumed the old map by Anaximander, complete with errors. It is true that Eratosthenes had neglected the stars in favor of the sun when taking his measurements, observing the shadow cast on a gnomon. A measuring tool that uses the shadow cast by the sun, such as the pin of a sundial, in Greek, gnomon literally means "the thing that reveals another." Is a man who is interested in the shadows on the ground or the angle of the sun in the bottom of a well truly reliable?

Let us return to Strabo, who boasted of having traveled the world. In his mind, a good geographer must be familiar with mathematics and physics, but he must, in particular, be a philosopher, as he suggests in the foreword to the first book of his encyclopedia *Geography*: "Yes, this is a philosopher's business, if there ever was a science, that is, the science of geography, the subject of this study… Moreover, the amount of knowledge that helps to perform this type of work well can only be found in a man who has a habit of taking into account both the divine and the human, whose knowledge is, by definition, philosophy. Also, the many benefits gained in such diverse fields and that touch political life and the practice of government, as well as an understanding of celestial phenomena, of the earth and the seas and all that they hold, of living beings, plants, fruit and the distinctive features of each country, requires the same kind of man, someone who cares about a way of life and happiness."

Hemispheric portolan chart of the Old World, from Europe to Africa and to India, drawn by Battista Agnese for the Guadagni family of Florence. (Circa 1540. The British Library, London.)

The very wise Ptolemy (90–168), who was mad about mathematics and physics, has every right to be called the father of geography. Equipped with ancient maps and observations made during his time, he corrected the errors of his predecessors and charted distances on Earth in degrees and minutes. Ptolemy used the degrees of longitude and latitude and submitted the position of places to astronomical observations. He thought that Eratosthenes erred in his calculations of the earth's circumference and set it at 17,895 miles (28,800 km), which made the world much smaller. Relying on Ptolemy's maps, Columbus would discover a land other than the one he was trying to reach.

In the 8th century, Ptolemy's map, which at the time was being used as a reference in the West, was corrected and completed by Arab geographers. Under the caliphate of Al-Ma'mun in Bagdad, the *jughrafiya* (an Arab word translated literally into Greek to give us the word "geography") occupied a place of honor, and Al-Khuwârizmî (780–850) would be as honored as Ptolemy. Al-Khuwârizmî was one of the first Arab geographers to show the shape of the earth in the form of a sphere, with its northern half divided into seven longitudinal bands starting from the equator. However, Ptolemy would not become familiar with the territories that would go on to become part of Islam. This new representation of the conquered lands would prove to be a new era in history.

Tabula orbis cum descriptione ventorum, a map of the world engraved on colored wood by Laurentus Frisius. (1541. From Martin Waldseemüller's edition of Ptolemy's Geography. Lyons, France. Private collection.)

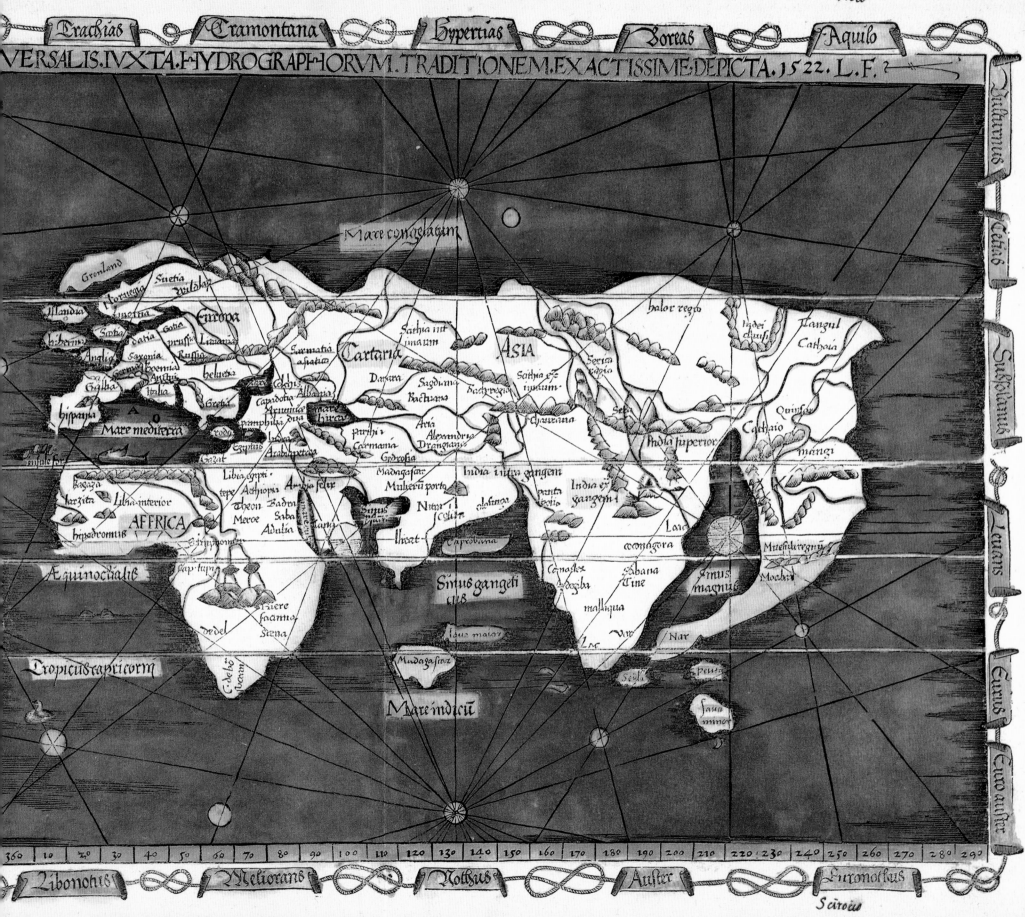

MAR DES

ZUR

MARE

PACIFICUM

a Ferd. Magellano dictum

Archipelagus

Insularum

de la Victoria

Sorlinges

Fretum Magellanicum

Super Eylanden

MAR DES

ZUR

NOVUM MARE

Vulgo

I. de Diego Ramires

a. S. Bartholome . Kruyck.   d. Æolus . e. Witte bay
b. S. Ierofme . Grotewal   f. Willems bay, g. Ridders bay. R.S.T.
'tgroot Pinguins eylandt.   h. C. de Nassou
c. Musflecove   i. Gr. Hendr. Fredricks bay
                          k. Onbequame bay
                          l. Ongeluckige bay   Nieuwe Straet
                          V. Een hooge bergh van
                          waermen de vorder ge-
                          brocken landen can sien

B. Gallego

Ir. Bergen

MAR

Fretum Magellanicum

DES

PATAGONVM

REGIO.

TIERRA

DEL FVOGO

C. de Pennas

C. de St Ines

Verschoors Ree

Mauritius Landt

Valetyns Bay

MAGELLANICA.

Nassausche Voerd

Lheremitens eylandt

I. de Gonçalo

AVSTR

Barnevelts Eylanden

C. Hoorn

TAI
MAGEL
QUA TIERRA
celeberrimis In
et I. Le Ma

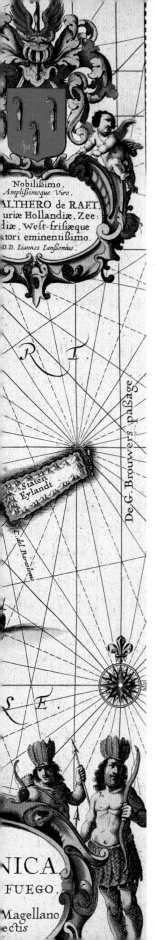

South America: Map showing the region of Tierra del Fuego, the tip of South America, and the Strait of Magellan by Juan Janssonio, Amsterdam. The strait was named after the navigator who was the first to take this natural passage between the Atlantic and Pacific oceans in 1520. The natives shown on the right side of the map are depicted as mythological figures on the left side. As for the surroundings, they appear perfectly inviting. (1666. The British Library, London.)

FOLLOWING DOUBLE-PAGE:
Stereographic projection of the map of the world (1848. The British Library, London.)

W hether lengthwise, widthwise or across, the world could henceforth be calculated, measured and divided into grids. Its image suddenly appeared like a giant graduated sheet of paper from which no place could escape. From that time on, the Earth was caught in a fishnet, a tightly meshed lattice. The ascendancy of human knowledge pit itself against the landscape and most distant horizons: each point of the globe could now be located. The intoxication of knowledge, the triumph of reason, the covetousness of the powerful and the madness of size could all be demonstrated by the mapped globe.

All that remained for the dreamers, those for whom straight lines evoke a desire to wander, were the tiny illuminations and figures drawn in the margins along maps: it is there that the imagination reassumes its rights. The dreamers also still had the history of Chinese cartography. Their maps were initially drawn on pieces of silk that had rectangular markings that would be nothing more than a transcription of the weft that served as their support: it is as if the silk weavers had been the first artisans to weave the fabric of the world.

Let us hope the dreamer still exist, there, here or somewhere! That nature reassumes its rights and that routes blur is rather reassuring. Otherwise, what would we have to dream about?

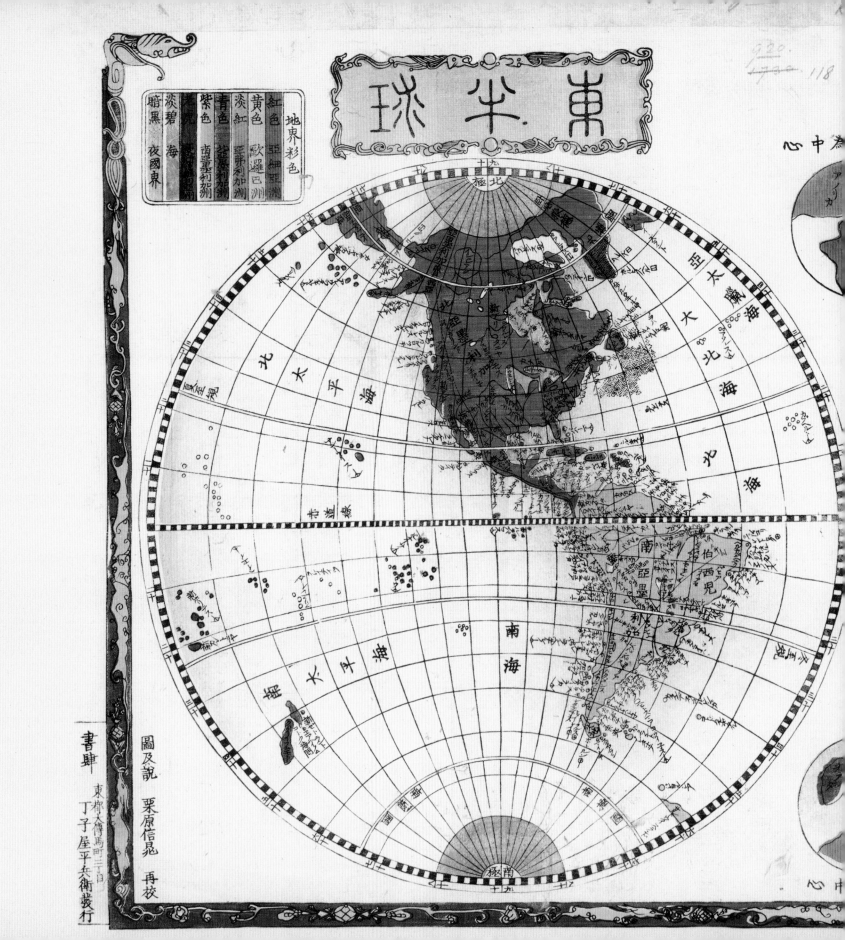

書肆　東都大傳馬町三丁目　丁子屋平兵衞發行

圖及說　栗原信晁　再校

Europe: View of the North Atlantic coasts (Spain, Portugal, Ireland, Scotland, Iceland and Labrador) from the Book of Idrography, *an atlas by Jean Rotz dedicated to Henry VIII. (1542. The British Library, London.)*

Blown by the Winds

During his long voyage back to Ithaca in *The Odyssey*, each time Odysseus lands on an unknown island he asks himself questions like "Where am I? Is this an inhabited place where grapes and wheat are grown? Do the people welcome strangers in the name of Zeus?" For him, any territory that did not meet the criteria of the known and civilized Greek world could only be barbarian.

The place where we come from serves as our reference point. It allows us to clear a route through the intertwined network of cultures, religions and social organizations of places with which we are not familiar. However, creating this reference point requires us to obtain a certain amount of knowledge or beliefs, which act as ideological anchors that help establish and justify our common knowledge and common identity.

In the Middle Ages, Europeans abandoned the calculations, measurements and grids of the Greek geographers, and in doing so they lost their mathematical reference points and had to choose other ones. Under Christian influence, they plunged into an ideological description of the world that had to agree with the precepts of faith. What Ptolemy (90–168) had patiently recorded on maps with the help of his predecessors, who were just as curious as he was about the surprising world, was soon displaced by pious imagery and maps that traced the routes of faith. And, since Paradise can only lie in the east — where Christ arose and where Jerusalem lies — from that moment on European maps were directed toward the east.

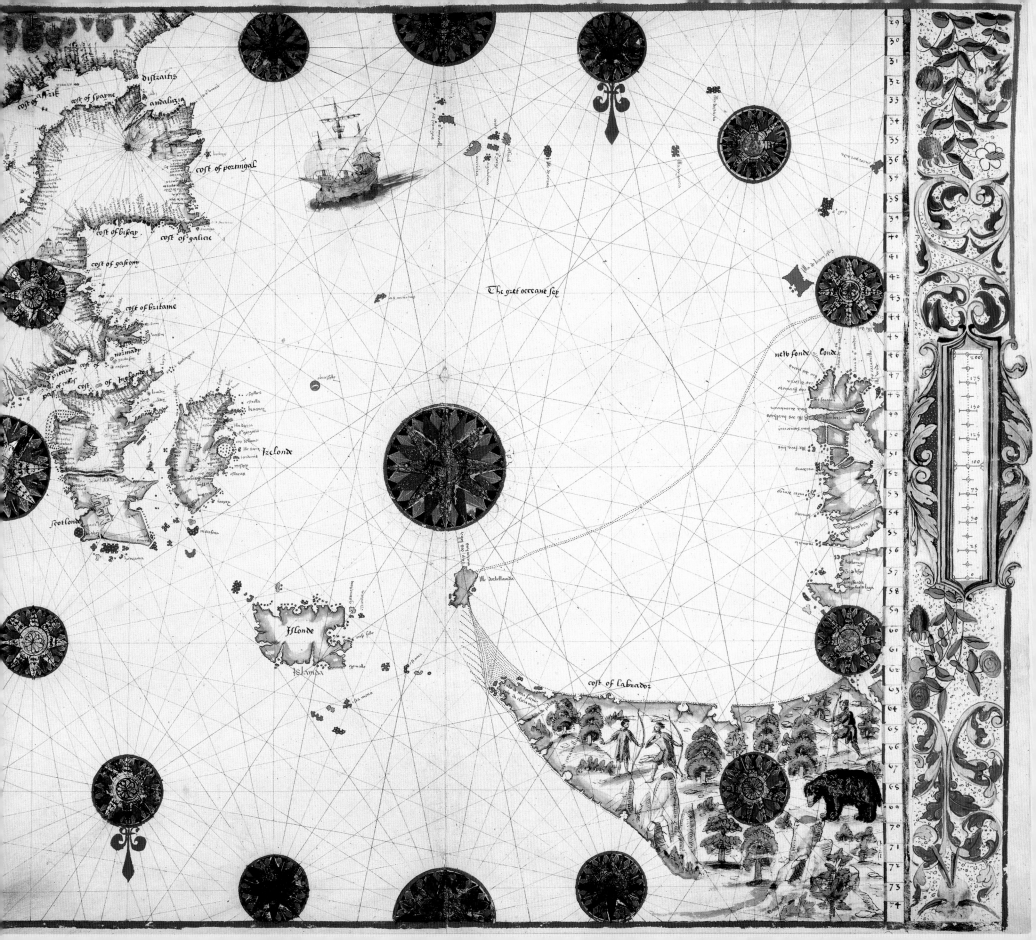

Legends and fables would always undermine the Earth of the geographers. In the Middle Ages, the Earth became a flat wheel where Europe and Africa occupied half of the world, and Asia alone occupied the other half. Knowledge lost its way in the imaginary lands and territories monstrously large or bursting with riches, and the spheres of the universe no longer turned smoothly. The knowledge gathered from the shadow of the Greek gnomons, from Eratosthenes and from the Egyptian geographers the Emperor Augustus brought to Rome disappeared, too often, in favor of spiritual salvation.

Literature has always traveled to improbable lands, from Plato's Atlantis, submerged in the ocean in the 10th century BCE, to Hsuan, the continent north of the China Sea governed by saints or fairies and described in the 1st century CE by the Chinese writer Tuo Tung-fang. But could readers, those sedentary travelers always ready to dream, really have believed such places existed because of the accuracy of the descriptions? By what trick of the mind did one believe in the craziest kingdoms, such as the mysterious Christian kingdom of Father John or Saint Brendan's Island of the Blessed? How could one take seriously and dread an invasion by Gog and Magog, Alexander the Great's two giants contained inside a wall? What happened so that the world of science that evolved over centuries was suddenly replaced by a fictional one? Wars, famines, plagues, beliefs, intellectual manipulation or political propaganda? And what needed to be done to allow a return from that period of traveling down the wrong road?

During his experiences with the Great Khan, his travels to China, Burma, Annam and India and his expeditions on the Silk Road, Marco Polo (1254–1324) visited places that would not be rediscovered until much later. The account of his adventures, *The Travels of Marco Polo*, written by Rustichello, includes numerous legends and wonders. The book was a huge success, and hundreds of handwritten copies circulated around Europe. The work soon became a reference source for merchants because it indicated the distances between cities in days and in miles. It also provided practical advice for traveling and doing business. But what was it really like out on the road?

Map of the Strait of Magellan with imaginary inhabitants, from Cosmographie Universelle *(Universal cosmography) by Guillaume Le Testu. (1555. Defense Historical Services, Ministry of Defense, Paris.)*

Did writings such as Rustichello's account of Marco Polo's travels motivate other adventurers to conquer new lands? And the merchants looking to expand the scope of their dealings but concerned about the safety of foreign lands or the navigability of routes, did they force geographers to reconsider the routes, coasts, ports and citadels on their maps? And did the pilgrims, stubborn in their propagation of the faith, provide mapmakers with accurate, practical indications? During the European expansion of the 16th century, the kings of Portugal and Spain divided the world between them, but they were obliged by the pope to convert the conquered lands and their unknown peoples to Catholicism.

No good route can be found without instruments, and the compass, which first came to Europe from China following the Arab conquests, may have helped the West head in a new, objective direction in the 12th century, at which time people began to abandon fantasies in favor of observation and correct measurements. The Chinese had their own rectangular grid system, similar perhaps to the scales of the tortoise whose shell they used for divination or, as some historians think, similar to the weft of the fabric on which they painted their maps. This system of representation was generally used to note places on an Earth they believed was flat.

Cartographers never stopped adapting to new information. However, it may have been the geomancers who, in their search to determine the positive and negative influences of a space in order to place people in harmony with nature, helped to discover the compass. The ancient Chinese treaties mentioned the presence of beneficial underground breezes traveling the earth in sinuous lines well before there was talk of magnetic forces. The geomancers used the compass, and they deduced that the heavens always point south, in the direction of the sun, of heat and of life.

Michel Culas in his *Grammaire de l'objet chinois* (Grammar of the Chinese object) proposes that the Chinese may have discovered the artificial magnet as early as the 1st century; others think that the first compasses, also called "governors of the south" were used as early as the 2nd century BCE. Whatever the case, this valuable navigational instrument made it possible for explorers to venture far from any coast, even when no stars were visible in the sky. The use of the compass became more widespread in the West beginning in the 13th century. Curiously, while the Asian compasses pointed south, with the needle pointing toward the South Pole, the most modern compasses have always preferred to follow the universal convention and reverse the directions. Thus, south is indicated by north. The magnetic north, geographical north, north to south — this is all it takes to get completely lost.

Europe. Wind rose taken from Première Œuvres (First works) by Jacques de Vaulx. (1583. National Library of France, Paris.)

Figure·Laquelle·demonstre

Selon le rumb de vent auquel lon aura sillé et fait chemin, pour auoir
esleué ou abaissé vng Degré de haulteur de latitude plus proche ou loing de
Lequinoctial Combien lon sera eslongé de lieues loing du meridien
ou ligne droicte du lieu dont lon est party

Autre Figure Par Laquelle Lon

Cognoistra Combien il conuient faire de lieues de chemin par quelque Rumd
demy rumd ou Cart de Rumd de vent que ce soit Pour esleuer ou abaisser vng degré
de haulteur de latitude loing ou proche de lequinoctial Ce qui se pourra voir
En posant la lidade dicelle figure dessus le Rumd de vent qu lon desirera scauoir

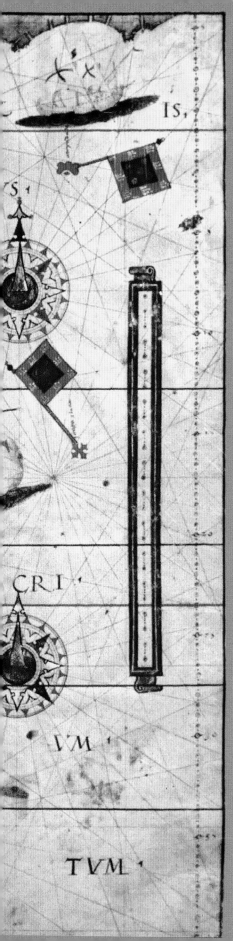

Until the 18th century, straight lines were drawn from the circle of the wind rose that decorated medieval maps. These lines allowed navigators to choose, from the start, the rhumb that suited them best and, once they were on the high seas, to determine their location by recording on the map the distance they estimated they had traveled in a given direction. Thirty-two rhumbs were recorded based on the four cardinal points — north, south, east and west — at an angle of 11°15'.

The oldest preserved Mediterranean portolan chart, the Carte Pisane, dates from the end of the 13th century and has two rhumbs drawn on it. On old maps such as this, the eastern rhumb is indicated by a cross, recalling the symbol used consistently throughout the Middle Ages for Christ and Jerusalem. This primary direction reminded navigators that every route has a spiritual path. The northern rhumb is often represented by a fleur-de-lis, and the reason is simple: while the English usually claim to be its creator, it was a French worker who made the first compasses, which were then copied by other nations. As for the mariner's compass, which the English also claim to have invented, they only translated the French name *compas de mer*.

This small patriotic correction, noted in Diderot and d'Alembert's encyclopedia, clearly demonstrates how the climate of scientific expeditions, supported by the kings of France and England whose maritime supremacy was undisputed, led to the rivalry between the Englishman James Cook and the Frenchman La Pérouse, between two colonial powers and between two national prides. Knowledge of the earth had become a political stake of great importance.

Brazil: Map drawn by the Portuguese navigators Pedro Reinel and Lopo Homem in 1525. The names of the ports are written vertically, and realistic birds and imaginary monsters decorate the map. As for the natives gathering wood, they prove that the forests of Brazil were easy to harvest and that there was no shortage of workers, as long as one negotiated with the tribal chiefs. (National Library of France, Paris.)

71

On the Road

"On the island, more or less everywhere, the journeys of tiny animals, the routes of insects and flying seeds, the passage of the wind, cool, hot, cold. It's a thin point of land, a point like millions of others, hardly similar, hardly different."

J.M.G. Le Clézio, The Book of Flights, An Adventure Story.

The Mediterranean Basin, the Black Sea, the Horn of Africa, the Arabian Peninsula and the Persian Gulf are all visible on the map drawn by Eratosthenes (circa 276–194 BCE). Beyond those areas, the lines are not as accurate and the space is lost to the unknown. For the horizon to one day become more familiar, it would take centuries of shipwrecks, of unfinished voyages, of uncertain routes taken at great risk and of wars, too, for war more often than the desire to know pushes man to take to the sea and to travel the roads. And there was no shortage of invasions, conquests and re-conquests during the Middle Ages. Not until the 16th century would an educated European be able to locate the continents in their proper proportions. The world map prepared by Ptolemy (90–168) would, however, prevail until the Renaissance.

We know that in 329 BCE Alexander the Great, who understood the importance of the Silk Road, reached an agreement with the Scythes that allowed caravans, which could hold 100 to 150 people, to travel freely. Later, the conquests of the new Roman Empire allowed Europeans to trade with China. Although this country remained somewhat unreal, distant and fantastical, it also provided luxurious fabrics worn by the wealthiest people. As early as the 1st century, a 4,350-mile (7,000 km) route linked China, Central Asia, Northern India and the Parthian and Roman empires. A little later, during the 3rd century, routes opened from China to India. Chinese authorities also understood the benefits to be gained from trading silk. Nonetheless, beginning in the 8th century, the Muslim conquests advanced, eventually reaching the rich city of Samarkand (in present-day Uzbekistan) and making the Silk Road dangerous and difficult.

During the 13th century, the Mongols invaded China and settled in a huge empire that stretched from Korea to Eastern Europe and included Tonkin, Burma and Persia. Old Europe trembled before this so-called race from the ends of the earth. Curiously, the Great Khan, living in Beijing, the capital he founded, encouraged strangers to visit his lands. Pope Innocent IV (1180–1254) sent legates, including Jean du Plan Carpin (1180–1252); Saint Louis, King of France (1214–1270), also sent the Great Khan messages. Both Innocent IV and Saint Louis piously hoped the Mongols would convert to Catholicism, stop their massacres and help drive back the Muslims. The merchants of Genoa and Venice financially supported the papal delegation because Islam stood in the way of the silk and spice trades.

Russia: "Russiae, Moscoviae et Tartariae Descriptio," an engraving from Abraham Ortelius's atlas. (1562. Library of the Decorative Arts, Paris.)

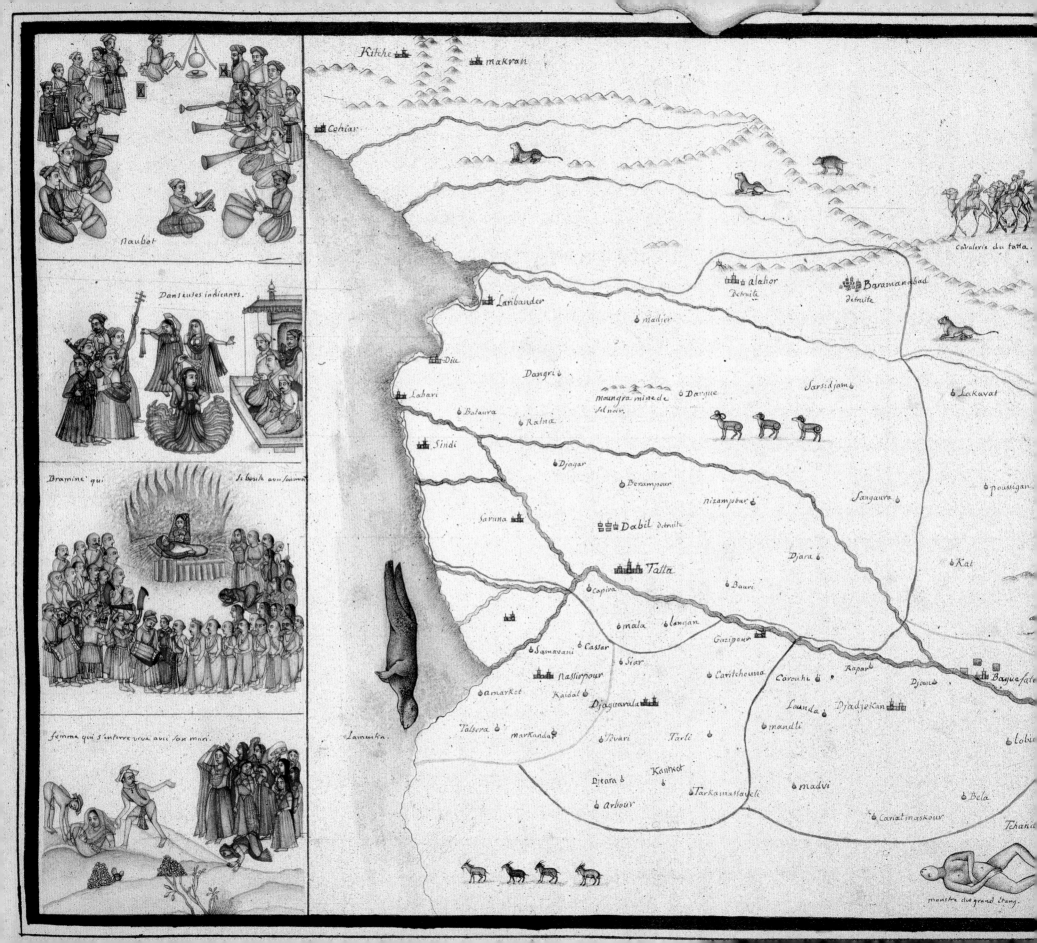

naubot

Danseuses indiennes.

Bramine qui   si brusle avec sa femme

femme qui s'enterre vive avec son mari.

Kitche

makran

Cohiar

Cavalerie du tatta

alahor
Detruite

Baramanabad
detruite

Laribander

madier

Diu

Dangri

Moungra mine de
sel noir.

Dargue

Sarsidjam

Lakavat

Lahari

Balaura

Ratna

Sindi

Djagar

Benampour

nizampbur

Sangaura

poussigan

Saruna

Dabil detruite

Djara

Kat

Tatta

Bauri

capira

mala

lançan

Gazipour

Rapar

Djoun

Bagiesate

Samavani

Cassar

Siar

Caritchouna

Carouhi

market

Nassirpour

Kaidal

Djaguavala

Djadjekan

Talsera

Markanda

Bvari

Tarti

Lounda

mandli

Lobie

Djeara

Kanhot

madvi

arbour

Tarkamassaveli

Bela

Cariatmaskour

Tchan

Lamuikin

monstre du grand etang

Suddenly China, as described by travelers, ambassadors and monks, was draped in colors: *There are cities surrounded by gold, by walls made of silver and ramparts made of gold.* On a more pragmatic note, they added: *Their land is rich in wheat, wine, gold, silk and in all things useful to human life.* The West dreamed of China's wealth.

The legends flourished, and Marco Polo fed them with his tales: thanks to the magic of the enchanters, cups full of wine and milk would be brought to the lips of the Great Khan each time he wanted to slake his thirst. Lions bowed, peacocks danced and parrots spoke so well they sounded like reasonable men. He also told of paper money, stones that healed or attracted rain, and others that burned all night — there were so many wonders, one could not name them all. Of course, one could also have lamented the steppe that needed irrigating or the uninhabited places. However, there were so many cities and inhabitants, Europeans thought everything could be perfect if the land and sea routes were safer, but pirates infested the China Sea, the Gulf of Bengal and the Arabian and African coasts. Since the route to the Far East went around Africa, it was no longer the Italians but the Portuguese who set off in their caravels on adventures.

At the end of the 14th century, the Mongols were driven out of China, and the land-based silk routes began to collapse. In 1453, when the Turks took Constantinople — the capital of the Byzantine Empire, which at the time was the greatest Christian power in the world — the West could no longer access the Black Sea and Asia Minor. From that moment on, Europeans sought to move their trading from the Mediterranean to the north and the Atlantic in order to develop their economies and expand their territories in the American and African continents. They thought increasingly of clearing a northeastern route to China by following the Siberian coast.

With the rich Italian merchants having being supplanted by the Portuguese, it was the latter who would supply Europe with Asian products and silk during the 15th and 16th centuries. However, in the 17th century their trading posts fell under the domination of the Dutch, who, in turn, were supplanted by the English. Nonetheless, the tales told by travelers, their sketches and their notes enriched the routes they traveled by populating them with unexpected people, animals and plants, leaving those who would follow in their footsteps an exotic elsewhere to dream about.

India: Map of Tatt, an Indian province of the Moghul Empire, which is today the Zind region in Pakistan. The map shows different scenes of cultural and religious traditions. It is from the Album de cartes représentant l'empire Moghul *(Album presenting maps of the Moghul Empire) by Colonel Jean-Baptiste Gentil. (1770. The British Library, London.)*

What was so interesting about the north that it attracted Norman, Portuguese and English sailors? It was otter and beaver pelts and fishing, for the ocean was teeming with fish. The Basques came to hunt whales.

In 1534, King Francis I of France sent Jacques Cartier to discover a western route to Asia. But the king also wanted to conquer some "islands and countries where there is gold and other riches." Cartier left with two ships and 61 men on his first voyage, three ships and 110 men on his second voyage and five ships and 1,500 men on his third voyage: given these numbers, it is easy to see that France was very much interested in colonization. Cartier set sail for the Gulf of Saint Lawrence by following the west coast of Newfoundland, which was already known and mapped. After sailing past the Magdalen Islands and Prince Edward Island, he reached Gaspé Bay where he erected a 30-foot (9 m) high cross, a religious and political symbol of settlement.

The Native Americans quickly understood his intentions, especially when he kidnapped the son of Chief Donnacona at Hochelaga and, soon after, the chief himself and took them both back to France.

From one end of the world to the other, the explorers' concerns were always the same: to bring back proof that supported their accounts of the riches and resources that could be exploited in the new lands. The legends would do the rest: in Cartier's case, it was the unbelievable kingdom of the Saguenay, thought to be rich in gold, which was, in reality, iron ore, and his tales of the Natives at Hochelaga, on the banks of the Saint Lawrence, who worshipped him as a healer with magical powers. However, the so-called white man's curse, smallpox, against which Native Americans were not immune, would ravage their population. And yet, with no ill feelings, they cared for Cartier's sailors suffering from scurvy.

Cartier reached the Gulf of Saint Lawrence, explored the bays and, in 1535, sailed 620 miles (1,000 km) up river. Eventually he discovered a village that he named Mont-Royal in honor of the king. In some ways, his cartography boasts of the hospitality of the Iroquois, so welcoming were they to the newcomers he named this new land Canada, believing in error that the Huron-Iroquoian word for village, kanata, meant territory. Subsequently, maps would assume this new name.

Jacques Cartier was impressed by the fortifications that protected the round city of Hochelaga, and he noted that the houses were made of wood bark. Lastly, he provided the necessary information about the environment, the habits and the customs of the inhabitants so that the French could settle this new continent.

In the 19th century, France was in full colonial expansion and reappropriated Cartier and Canada as emblematic of French genius and its hold on the New World. Painters, in turn, glorified the French discovery by showing Jacques Cartier being greeted by Native Americans. The myths of "unknown lands" and of natives welcoming civilization with open arms lasted a long time.

ABOVE AND OPPOSITE:
Greenland. Noorder dell van Europa, *volume 1, with a second page showing the title in French:* Le gran et nouveau atlas de la marine hydrographique dans lequel est compris et démonstré toutes les côtes du monde connu *(The big and new atlas of marine hydrography that comprises and shows all the coasts of the known world), by Gerard Van Keulen, Amsterdam. (1716. Municipal library, Versailles.)*

Verſche Riv:

Arcticus

C: Kieritt

E R E "

Soloſki Eyl:
Zalotitza

Witte

Zee

Wieli

Cſcat

Warſi

longy

za

C. Bona Fortuna

C. Pentecoſt

Mezeenſche Golf

Iampas

Soma

Cattnoes

de Dwina

Moedeskee Cruijs Eijland

L. Archangel

St Nicolaas

Tijsers Eijland

Poda Oijl

Ouchmawoloch

Nieuwe

t'Noorder d

Sijnde see

Groenlandſe en

i n l a n d

Aſpo

Tavaſtehr

Novoſloti

Peſtras

Corfnes

Wiborgh

Fiorkolwidn

Steijkludde

Kranitza

Siſtorbjk

Nyens Skantz

Kexholm

Sordowalla

Vzio

Lungula

Koudova

Ladoga Zee

Tullaſa

Happuna

Sivabak

Woronia

Stralba

Rattefarri

Karisvalla

Coporie

Tourvala

Novogorod

Cexorio

Narva

Rabelhaeſt

Carel

Kexo

Rabelm

L Y F S A N D

On a Global Scale

Landscape Images

"Without a doubt, it would be possible, like the one used to analyze the different periods in painter's career (blue or pink, figurative or abstract), to distinguish in the life of Parisians' successive 'periods,' for example, a Montparnasse period and a Bonne-Nouvelle period. To each one there corresponds (as we know all too well), a more secret geography: the map of the subway is also a map of tenderness or the open hand that one must know how to fold and to examine to clear a passage for the line of the head to the line of the heart."

Marc Augé, *In the Metro*

For American novelist Paul Theroux, it is possible to see the artist Mondrian in his final period in the plan of the London Underground by screwing up one's eyes while looking at it. But how does one go from a map to a plan, a micro-world already so sufficiently complex that the memory fails while trying to remember it? The cartographers of the New York subway system have already revised its plan three times so that it can be read by all, whether resident or visiting. In Calcutta, where 15 million people live, only one line crosses the city from top to bottom, which clearly simplifies the job, but it also shows the dire circumstances of the infrastructure. In Tokyo, the numbering of places poses a problem because time, as well as space, is taken into account. For the inexperienced, the numbers seem to follow one another completely randomly. This transforms every citizen of Tokyo if not into a cartographer, at least into a map expert. The map is sketched on a piece of paper and sent to the person one is meeting because only the mail carrier knows the true address. Others are happy to have a few permanent markers instead: a statue, a main thoroughfare, a store. (Although the best thing is to be escorted to a destination.)

This recalls the problems men of the ancient world faced when trying to establish indicators that could be understood by those who would bend over their maps. There were the natural signs — the sun, the moon, the stars, the mountains and the rocks — to which were added codes and cultural signs. Such codes and signs are the ancestors of the symbols commonly found on modern maps, which are supposed to be easily decipherable and form a network of universal signs that can be understood regardless of where one is on the planet. In response to the green of the earth, the blue of the sea, the meandering of the rivers and the curves of the mountains, there are the crosses of the churches, the towers of the kingdoms and the ships that cross the oceans. It is the poetry of a miniature world that is reassuring on a human scale, where the fear of getting lost disappears.

PRECEDING DOUBLE PAGE: *Canada: Detail from a portolan chart drawn by Pierre Desceliers in 1536 or 1542 that shows Jacques Cartier and his companions in Canada, where the land is arable and the inhabitants are welcoming. (The British Library, London.)*

Mountains and Marvels

Hills and mountains: before these were transformed into the triangle-shaped symbols we see on today's maps, cartographers liked to show their rounded summits and curvy outlines by suggesting a third dimension in the flat world of atlases. Should one see these mounds on paper as an extension of the beliefs that made Olympus, Sinai, Mount Thabor, Elbrouz and Fuji-Yama places of divine revelation?

According to the aesthetic canons in effect in Japan from the end of the 16th century to the 18th century, people wanted to see the landscape on the map. The rich daimyos (feudal barons) decorated their homes with monumental and sumptuous maps. The artists who created them introduced recurring themes in Japanese painting, called yamato-e, in which mountains — rounded, snowy or in the clouds and shining with gold and silver powder — symbolize, through the richness of the pigments used, the splendor of Japan and its attachment to Fuji-Yama, the home of the gods. From the Buddhist temples to the Shinto sanctuaries, every potentate felt he deserved to have a map of his own.

In the 19th century, the Himalayan monasteries in the Zanskar Valley joined the trees and animals in the heart of the mountain, and the representations of Buddha rose as high as the summit of the mountains. Piety imagined thusly can be mapped.

More than a physical reality, the landscape reproduced on maps must be read as a symbolic representation of space. Some elements are emphasized more than others. One has to know how to decode a map based on the size and hierarchy of its elements to fully understand it.

Zanskar Valley, the Himalayas:
Collection of maps of Tibet and the
Ladakh region. (Between 1844 and 1862.
The British Library, London.)

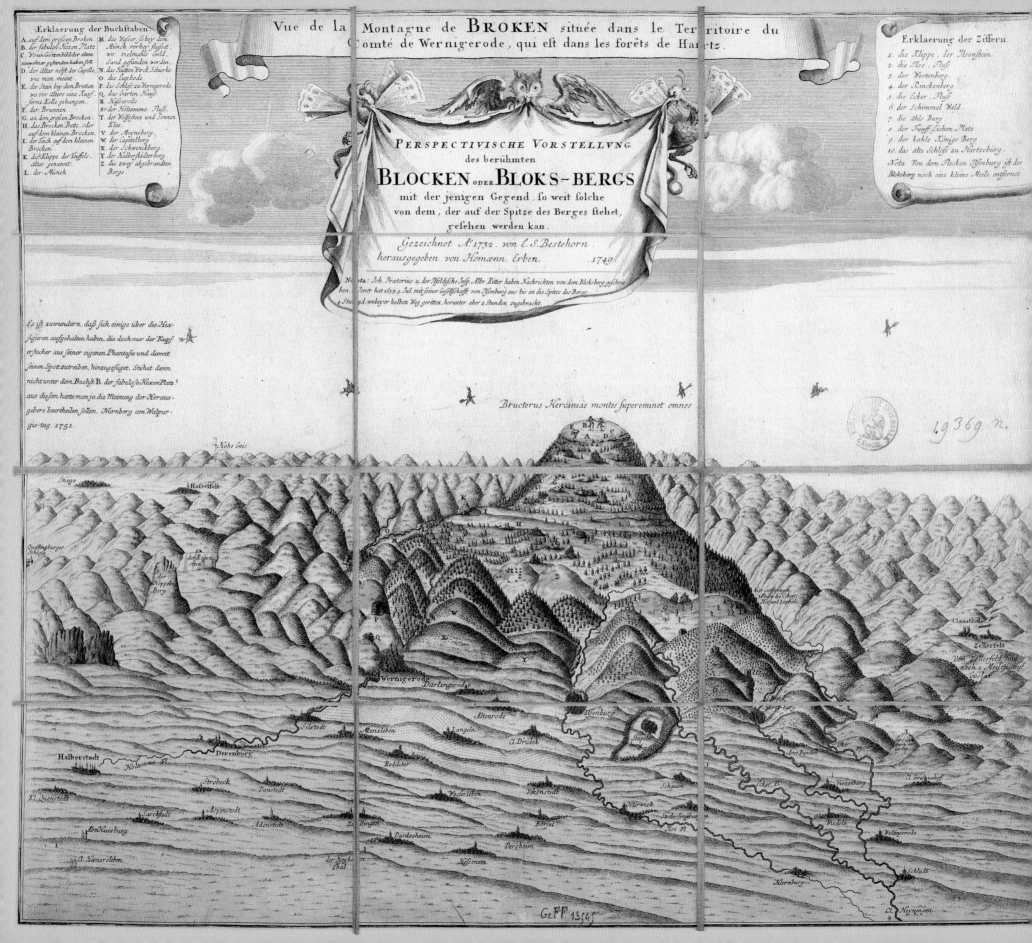

A German map from 1749 shows how Broken Mountain seems to structure the group of villages of the county of Wernigerode. The mountain appears to be the axis of an almost autonomous world that corresponds to pre-1871 Germany, before it became a truly unified state, when the territories lay side by side and each had a separate history. The hills that border the mountain appear to be as organized as the administration of this region of Saxony — a metaphor for a state within a state, where everything appears reasonably and permanently positioned. It is certainly a deceptive image because the map, a political vector just like any other, maneuvers and steers a delicate course. A map is often commissioned by its sponsor for an obliging reader, and it favorably impresses those who look at it.

As it is presented in the 15th century, mountains are only ever seen side by side with bishops and churches, demonstrating a clear desire to symbolize ecclesiastical power.

Germany: The inscription on the map, which appears in both French and German, reads "View of Broken Mountain located in the territory of the county of Wernigerode, which is in the Hartz forests." (1749. National Library of France, Paris.)

As for the history of landscape in cartography, it followed the evolution of the graphic arts. In Antiquity, painters only reproduced landscapes in the background of their frescoes. The meaning of the principal scene was more important than its surroundings, which remained anecdotal. During the Renaissance, the landscape started to assume more and more space in paintings and began to extend beyond the frame. There was the landscape painted in the classical manner — like an ideal nature tamed by man — which can be distinguished from the landscape of the naturalist. The latter style could, however, be grandiose and rich like that of Rubens or Rembrandt, or it could be topographic, that is, accurate and identifiable.

During the 18th century in the Netherlands, the naturalistic style influenced the way in which landscapes were reproduced on maps. At the time, no distinction was made between painting techniques and those of mapmaking. While previously mapmakers only seemed concerned with noting the elements that made up maps, from that time on they sought to re-transcribe these elements while respecting the geographical reality. The oblique view was replaced by a certain verticality. Scale, realistic shape and direction became a priority for artists. In France, civil or military engineers, accustomed to topographical landmarks, would transform prestigious maps into functional maps. Artistic imagination lost ground to practicalities.

Indonesia: Indonesia became a Dutch colony in 1602. On this map the Moluccas islands are shown as active volcanoes. (1646. The British Library, London.)

ÍLHAS·DE

ALVCO·

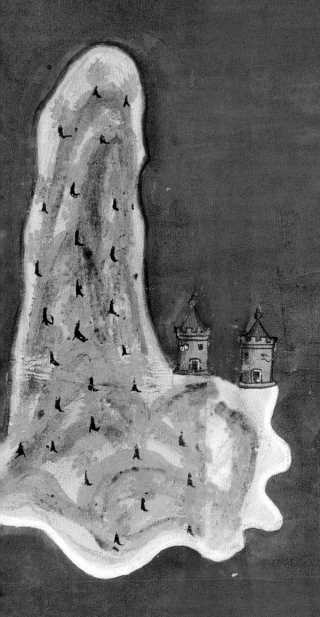
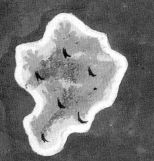

The Glory of the Kingdom

Points, lines and surfaces: these are what make up a road map today. The points serve to circumscribe natural landmarks or towns. The lines provide an indication of distances and the shape of rivers, highways or roads. The surfaces can represent large cities, parks or forests. These maps show scale and sizes through visual variables. The points and the circles expand and shrink based on the elements they represent. It is a rationalized hierarchy, which is similarly demonstrated in a 16th-century painting of the city of Nuremberg. The city was in full economic expansion, and it is shown in the middle of the forest, isolated and proud behind its fortress. The city grew in influence when Emperor Sigismund entrusted it with the protection of the Treasury, the royal insignia, the crown jewels and a collection of relics. A commercial hub, the city was also located at the center of numerous trade routes to the Balkans, Vienna, Antwerp, Venice, Prague and Strasbourg.

Germany. View of Nuremberg with the Sebald and Lorenz forests, *by Erhard Etzlaub. (1515. Germanisches National Museum, Nuremberg, Germany.)*

ABOVE: *Constantinople, Turkey:* Liber insularum *by Cristoforo Buondelmonti, a religious Florentine who traveled through Greece for several years. (Second half of the 15th century. National Library of France, Paris.)*

OPPOSITE: *China: This image is taken from a map of the world by Fra Mauro, an Italian priest and cosmographer who was famous in his day. (1449. Marciana National Library, Venice, Italy.)*

E lsewhere, in another time, everyone was still proud of the emblematic or real greatness of their city, ready to roll out the entire space of the atlas in order to show the extent of its place in the world. The castles burst with pride, and standards blew in the wind. On maps the cities invaded the countryside, and the villages, although much bigger than the cities, were relegated to the edges. It was not so much a question of cartography, but of politics; the relationships were not proportional. In his book *Héros et merveilles du Moyen Âge* (heroes and wonders of the Middle Ages), the medievalist Jacques Le Goff notes that in the European imagination, the fortified castle is highly symbolic and proves that the feudal system was a fundamental stratum of material and social realities from the 10th century to the French Revolution. In Le Goff's estimation, the castle is an image of strength and power. It recalls an era when war was everywhere and when the principal hero, besides the saint chosen by the grace of God, was a warrior who distinguished himself through the prestige of his home before he distinguished himself through his prowess.

Questo excellentissimo e
potentissimo iperador el qual
ha .lxx. re de corona soto el suo
dominio quado el ua a spaso
el senta i un caro doro e dauo
lio ornado de coie el priesio
le qual e iextimabile. e ques
caro uie menado dauno ele fan
te biacho. e ha .iiii. re di piu ndili
del suo regno uno per canton
che regeno questo caro. e li al
tri li uano auanti .con assai
numero de homeni darme da
uanti e dadriedo e qui sono
tuti i piaceri gentileçe ecostu
mi del mõdo.

zianglu

CHATAIO

Ponte mira
rze archi e sien
i qual tanti
telli. apun
sup el qual
me polisan

Archanara

f.l. polisan
chin

P.
mi
le.

IMPERIO e tri
umpho no
bilissimo
del chataio

châbaleç

c

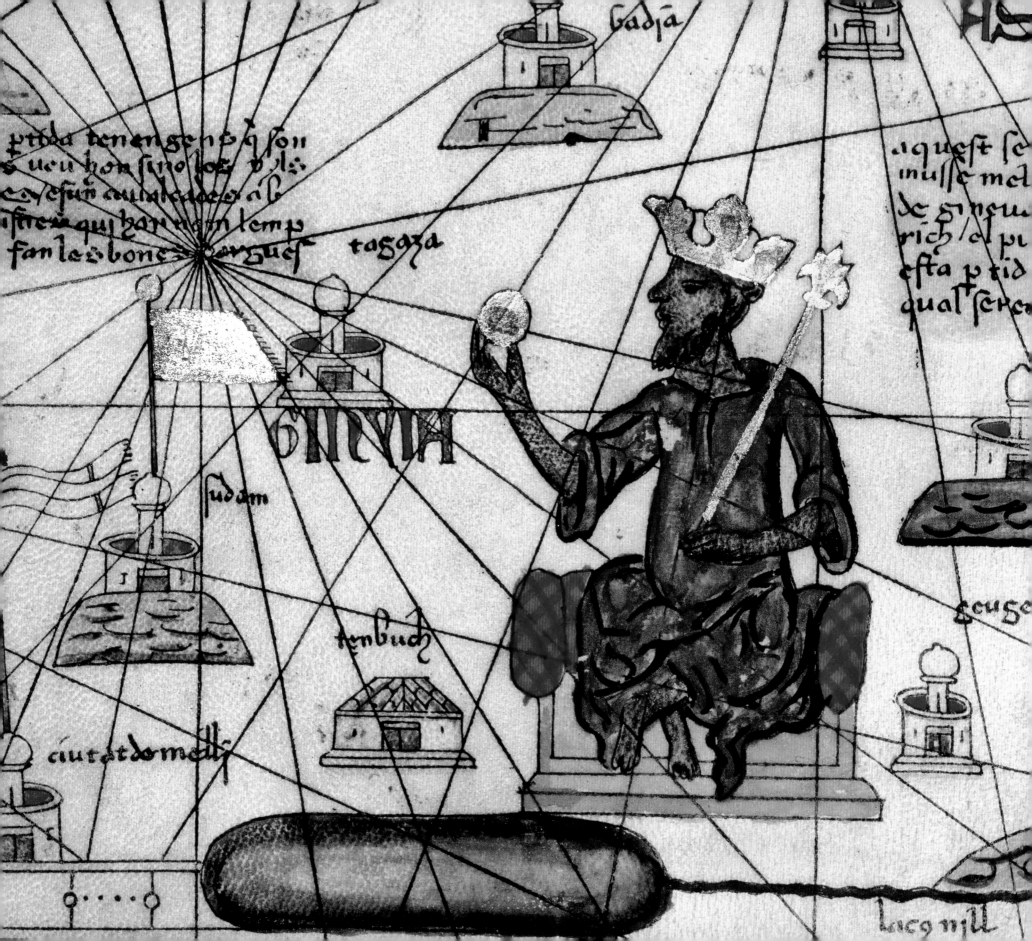

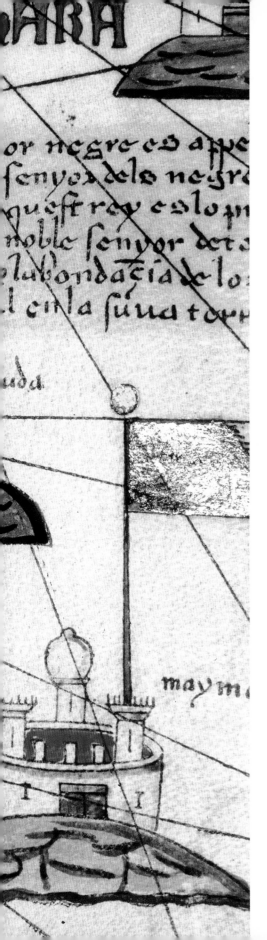

Beginning in 1595, Gerardus Mercator tried to take a census of the princely capitals in his atlas, thus offering a vast panorama of the nobility. Prior to that atlas, Abraham Cresques' famous *Atlas Catalan* (1375) indicated on velum the misadventures of the first travelers. Cresques took his inspiration from, among others, the accounts of Marco Polo. Manda Mussa, the king of Mali, also occupies an important place on one of the sheets. He is holding a golden seed in his hand and is surrounded by little mosques or palaces. His crown and his scepter shine intensely. The sovereign was very rich, as proven by his expedition to Mecca in 1324, during which he was escorted by 15,000 to 60,000 men and 500 slaves, while 40 mules transported as much gold as possible. Cresques produced his atlas at the height of exchanges between the Malian king and Europeans, particularly the Portuguese, but also between the king and Maghrebians. Maghreb (a region of northwest Africa that includes present-day Morocco, Algeria and Tunisia) was an important center for Arab poets, scholars, professors and physicians.

The history of maps shows the scope of political, social and religious powers. It was a "science of princes" in which one finds the nobility's cultural codes, whether they were European monarchs, rulers of Chinese dynasties, Moghul emperors, caliphs or sultans.

*Africa: The King of Mali. "Asia in the 13th century,"
a detail from the* Atlas Catalan *by Abraham
Cresques. (1375. National Library of France, Paris.)*

Lay of the Land

Researchers found a clay tablet from 2300 BCE, which demonstrates that people have been preoccupied with identifying land since Antiquity. It was necessary to record cultivated land, but mapping land also became a step that was needed in order to calculate the tax to be paid to the royal treasury. Well before the Greek system of Ptolemy, which involved placing the sphere of the earth in a network of longitudes and latitudes, the Chinese had established a system of coordinates, which they used to establish how land was divided and where it was located. When they applied their calculations to create a map that was drawn to scale, it was immediately accurate because the data had already been collected and recorded over a long period time.

China: Map of the city of Suzhou, renowned for its bridges, canals, pagodas and gardens. (1229. The British Library, London)

平江圖
北

MACAO

In 15th-century France, painters played a role in the preparation of "judicial" maps. These maps served as proof in the event of litigation concerning an inheritance, and litigators were strongly recommended to bring a figurative example or portrait that showed the location of the inheritance as closely as possible at the trial.

The word "portrait" would also be used to designate views of cities. The "lively portrait" or "true portrait" meant that the entire city was painted based on direct observation. This style is called chorography and is one of the techniques, along with topography, used by geographers. Chorography allows one to visualize the height and importance of the buildings, and from that perspective one can show the city's depth by drawing the streets between the houses. The ramparts were depicted as the principal structures, and a key at the bottom of the portrait identified them. There was no scale, but there was often an indication of the orientation of the map. The maps of provinces would also follow this same style. The point, therefore, was to show the distinct markings, such as urban areas, rivers, arable land, mills, bridges and the like. Recorded on a map, the data helped to emphasize not only the wealth of a country, but also the merit and knowledge of its inhabitants.

In France, the Church would also have its maps — those of the dioceses — because, much like an army, it needed to fight, to combat the devil wherever he may be and to defend its parishioners. As for the royal geographers, such as Nicolas de Nicolay (1517–1583), who received the order from Catherine de' Medici to describe the entire kingdom of France, they would have liked to have been able to access towers in order to better measure the relief of the countries and to better describe the distances between places. Changes in the way a territory was viewed continued with military cartography, which was handwritten rather than printed because it was confidential. Ramparts, fortifications, fortresses and the defense system all needed to be painted to show the details observed on the spot as accurately as possible and to create entire maps. Spying flourished as attempts were made to understand the intentions of the enemy, for military maps were drawn by civilian painters. They were also the best interpreters of their maps since they knew the territory.

Macao: Map by Pedro Barreto de Resende that groups together the Portuguese colonies located in eastern India. (1646. The British Library, London.)

It was only from the 17th century and into the 18th century that a smaller world began to appear on maps. More than just indicating position, maps henceforth served to record and to classify. They were given new functions, notably economic, which predated the arrival of thematic maps.

In atlases and magazines of the 19th century, geographers proposed a synthesis of human activities as well as of social and cultural distinctions. But, in the interim, in order to go from the map to the plan, from the territory to the piece of land, new methods and more accurate instruments were needed. Once these instruments were available, the nobility had to allow their properties to be surveyed so that maps could be drawn to scale. Protocols were created to gather the information, surveyors traveled the countryside and the cadastral map appeared.

An English guide, *The Complete Surveyor* (1685), recorded the lessons of this highly sought-after profession. For their part, tenants such as farmers disapproved of such precise mapping since it seemed to favor the owners, who benefited by readjusting their leases. The maps were decorated with the names of fields, paths, woods, orchards or tiny streams. One's heritage was thereby enclosed by force. Counties, regions, provinces and smaller spaces were mapped, and this fervor contributed to the prosperous business of map engravers. From the earth to the sky, roads and cities — everything — was set out in the form of globes, posters or atlases. In Kashmir, attempts were made to show a miniature world on tapestries. Trees, houses, animals, lush plants and canals were used to represent the city of Srinigar, long considered the "Venice of India."

Kashmir: Tapestry that represents the city
of Srinigar, with its vegetation and canals.
(19th century. Victoria and Albert Museum.
London, England.)

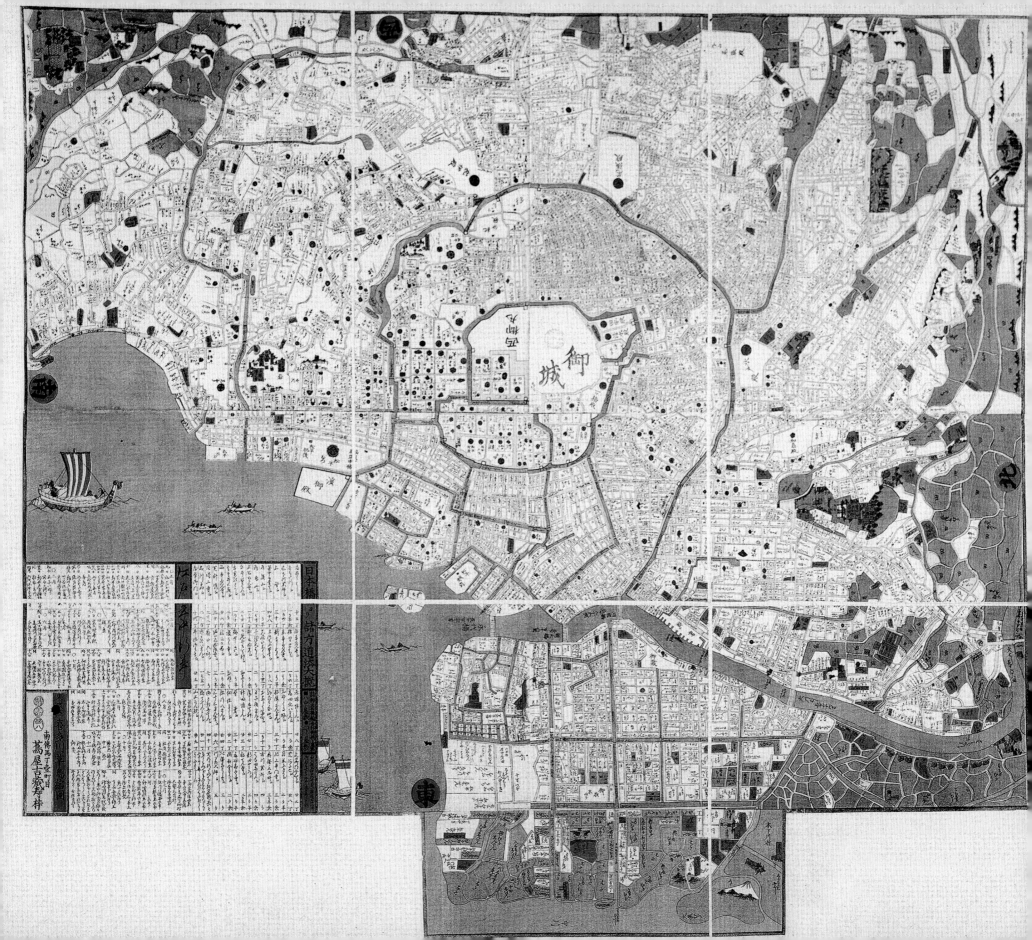

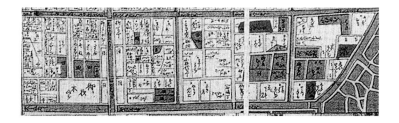

Since maps are at the heart of a power strategy, city plans, too, lie by omission. They show the main thoroughfares cleared of traffic, and the streets appear spacious. The movement of people and goods appears to be flowing continuously. Without a sense of vertical height, cities are hopelessly flat. They are also neutral because they only rarely include social data, such as the ethnic composition of the population. It would never occur to a cartographer, working under the orders of a sponsor, to paint a watercolor and, with the same precise brush, show the poor neighborhoods, disreputable alleys and monuments in ruins.

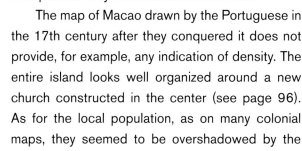

The map of Macao drawn by the Portuguese in the 17th century after they conquered it does not provide, for example, any indication of density. The entire island looks well organized around a new church constructed in the center (see page 96). As for the local population, as on many colonial maps, they seemed to be overshadowed by the new ruling class. In the Irish countryside of the 17th century, surveyors paid by English owners simply "forgot" to reproduce the houses of the natives of the region, although their maps did not lack other details. The silence of maps and plans can say a lot about political and religious tensions. However, as much as one might try to close, confine, print and distribute it, even the most humble territory seems to be a space in a state of perpetual change.

Japan: Plan of Tokyo. (1704. The British Library, London.)

Following the Flow

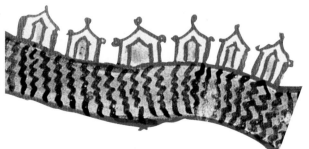

Whether a rain stick, the fountain of youth, voodoo worship in Haiti, Mami Wata worship in Togo, a siren or a sacred hippopotamus, from the spring to the river, imagery linked to water is present in all civilizations. It can be found in the reproductions of the world from earliest Antiquity, when in Egypt the hieroglyph for water was the sinuous line of the wave.

Iraq (Mesopotamia): The Tigris and the Euphrates from the atlas by Al Istalhry. (10th–11th centuries. Egyptian National Library, Cairo.)

From the Semites to the Pacific peoples and from the myth of Atlantis to the legends of the Andes, many mythologies talk about floods. These occurred frequently, reminding humans that the pact made with the gods had not been kept. To being again, to rebuild, to be reborn: this is what might cyclically await them.

102

MAPPING THE WORLD

صورة الجزيرة

الدجلة

الفرات

الزاب الاصغر

الزاب الاكبر

نهر الخابور

دجلة

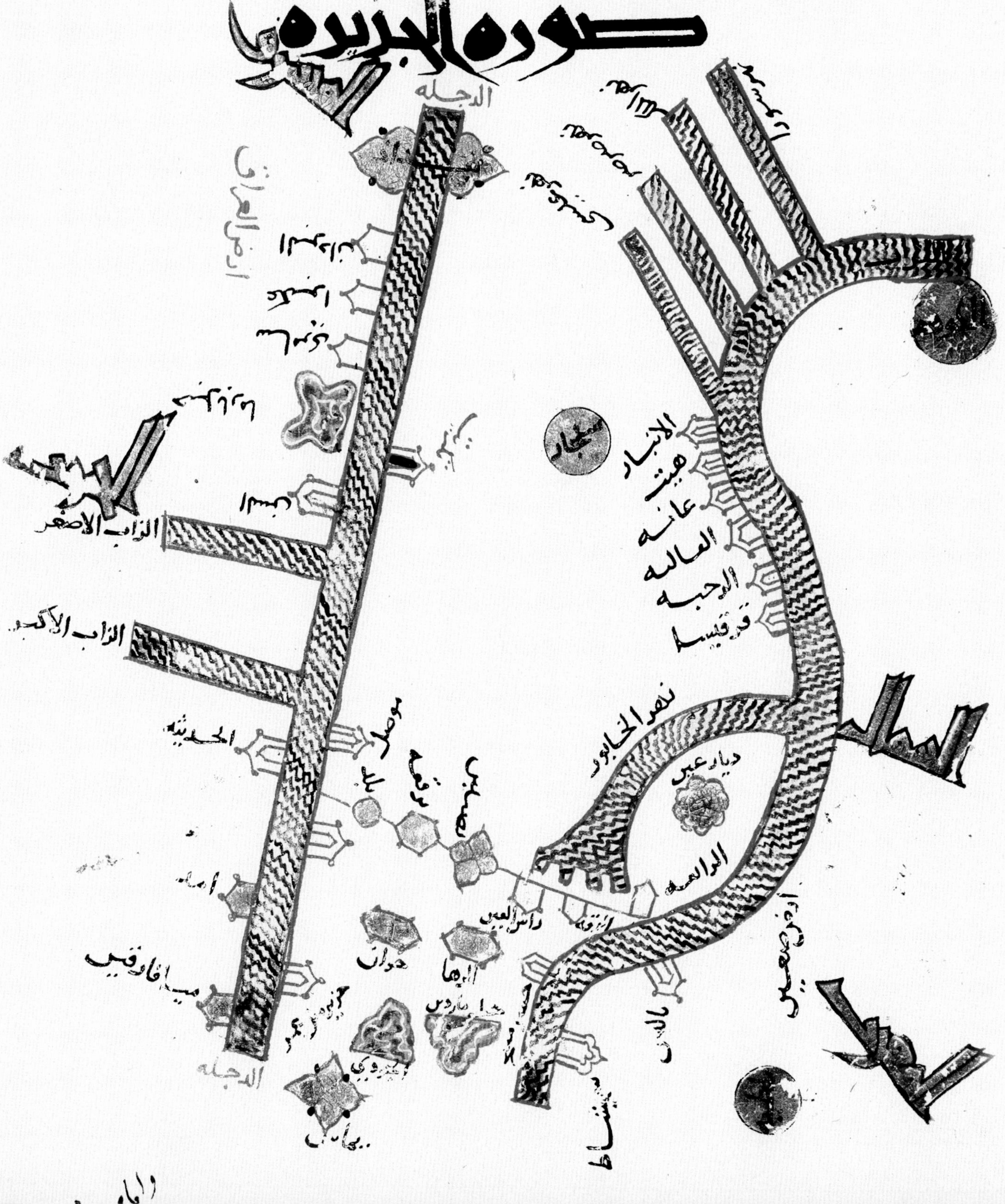

Mexico: Lienzo de Tetlama *(Linen of Tetlama),*
a map of rivers. (19th century. National Library
of France, Paris.)

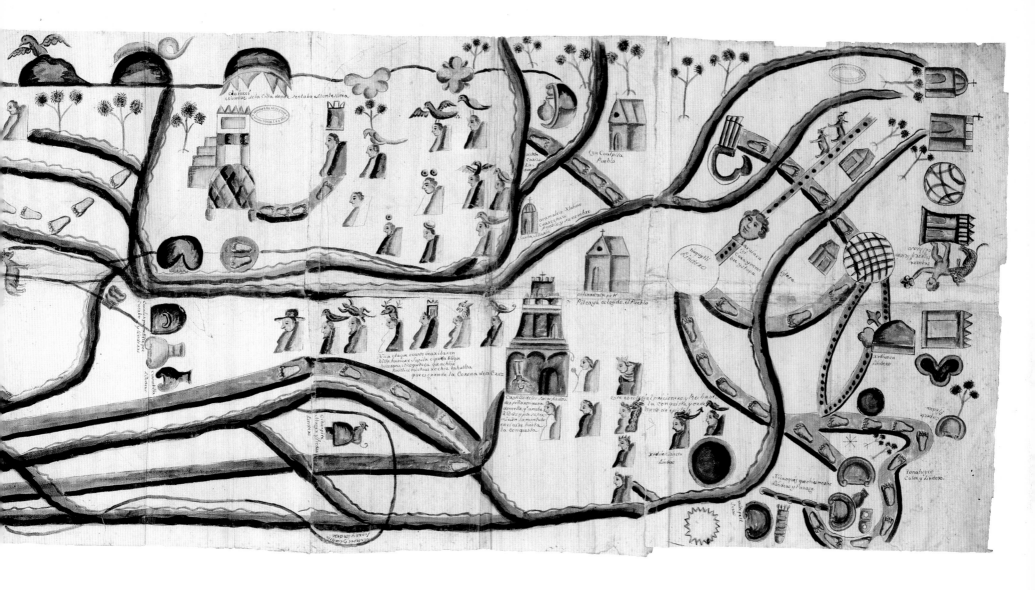

The Mexican mythology says that after the age of the successive suns comes the age of the water-sun, which floods the earth and changes humans into monkeys. Whether it is worshipped or feared, and whether it is shown as sea, river, ocean, lake, swamp, torrent, wadi or simple brook, water flows from the planispheres and maps of the world. Until the 13th century, water encircled representations of the sphere of the known world — the three continents then known, Europe, Asia and Africa — like a blue belt. A little later, the maps were crisscrossed by great oversized rivers of varying colors, as the colors of water can vary. Depending on the amount of mud or silt it carried along, the river was painted brown, red, green or blue. Water is a symbol of birth and life, and magical powers are often attributed to rivers.

In Tibet, there is no need for topographical symbols: the horn of the yak, a totemic animal, indicates where the herds can be watered and a camp can be set up. Elsewhere, springs were not often shown on old maps because it was believed they had supernatural origins, such as the Nile being conceived in a cave or the Ganges being linked with the hair of Shiva.

Therefore, it is not surprising that humans often settled alongside springs at the point where they became rivers. In Niger, the name of the River Djoliba, which crosses the country to the sea, means "the great blood," and it is this primordial water that slakes the thirst of all creatures along its path. More than 3,000 years before our time, many civilizations were born on the banks of rivers where they headed into the sea. These rivers played a prominent role in people's attempts to understand the world.

Chinese cartographers liked to evoke the expeditions along the 3,395-mile (5,463 km) long Huang He, the Yellow River, which gave structure to the empire and around which the Shang and Zhou dynasties established themselves. Beginning in Mongolia, the Yellow River fertilizes the great plain that stretches across northern China to the Yellow Sea. According to the ancient beliefs, the first and mythical Emperor Yu possessed the power to tame the gods of the river, the terrible dragon-kings, which terrorized the population with floods. In Rome, the Tiber was nicknamed the "father of all rivers." As for the Christians, they gave rivers a prominent place in Paradise in their depictions of the universe.

The purpose of hydrography is to measure and describe the depths of expanses of water and to show them on a map. The art of carrying out hydrographic surveys is very old. Before hydrographers could take measurements using the sound waves emitted by a sonar transmitter-receiver, they carried out surveys by hanging a lead weight overboard, and then they gathered information and noted the locations of buoys on nautical charts.

Damiata. is not Pelusium. but the next port of Nilus onto it to=
wards the west. w[hi]ch is also called Tanis. but this is not Tanis
for that Tanais is adioyning to Gosen. the same wher Ieremy was
stoned to death, & w[hi]ch the hebrews call Ioan. & hats also the name
of Bais. & now Sibnit.

r. 30

Melr: gml:

Egypt: The Nile Delta.
(1608. The British Library, London.)

Pelusium. the scrip=
tures call Sin, & Libi=
na, saith Montanus.
others take it for
Caphtor. Castaldus &
Zieglerus think it is
Damiata. Ang: Curio
saith y[a]t it is now Bil=
bin. Ortelius Tenes=
se: others, Belbais.

Babilon, the Arabians
call Mazar. the Chal=
deans Alkhaby r. Ioseph
Ierusolin; the Hebrews
Mizraim. Cairo stood
on the west side of it &
are now become one
Citty, saith Brochard.

Heliopolis, ther are too
Cities of y[a]t name, the
one on the edg of the
inferior Egypt, the other
surnamed metropolis
standeth farther nouth,
the scriptures call it On. gen. 41. Esai. 19.
p: Mela l. 63. r. 9. & plinie
l. 5. r. 9. call it polis
opidum. Melr: Guilandinus,
call it Bethsemes,
Tyreus, Malber. the
Arabeans, Bahalbeth.
Simeon Sethi, Solis fons.
Bethsemes. in Iosua 15. 19. 22.
kings, 1. 6. kings. 4. 14. par. 1. 3. 2. 25. 29.

Memphis built by Apis saith Aristippus
in 2[o] i books of y[e] Arcadien historye
therfore Aristeus argiuus called it
Sarapidis. & Apis was 2[o] third from
Inarus.

Heracleotiu ost.
Bolbitiu. ost.
Sebennitiu ost. et pharmuthiacu:
Pineptimi et pseu= =dostomu et Athri= bitzus flu:
Diolcos.
Pathmetru ost. et Busiritanu flu.
Mendesiu ostiu.
Tanis or Damiata.
Tanitiu fl.
Gerrion
Pelusiacum.
Erup: sirbonis.
ostiarine.
Damiarung

mereli
pathnam[us]
Cassie
CASIOTIS
Antheloni
Sirbo=
larius
panephi sis
pelusiu

Butos
Cabasa o
Xoies
panebethus
Tanis soanor
Bais. metropoly of A[g]
in Abrahams t[y]

Taua.
Leontopolis
GOSEN

Andropolis
Ramasse from wh[ich]
moses took his iur[ny]
for canaan

Heliopolis
or oni built
by Bunsidis.

Babilon. or Cairo.
Hero
traianus: f.

Memphis.
Saon.
Heriopolls. or. Aphropa
after the Arabeans. or
the read Iou. or sinus Arabicus
between thes
to mountains
moses march=
ed. in the
plajn of Pihahiroth

Baalse phon
the ten
teu of

Nilopolis

Cynopolis

Lycopolis

Panopolis

Coptos. a mart
towne of the Arabians.

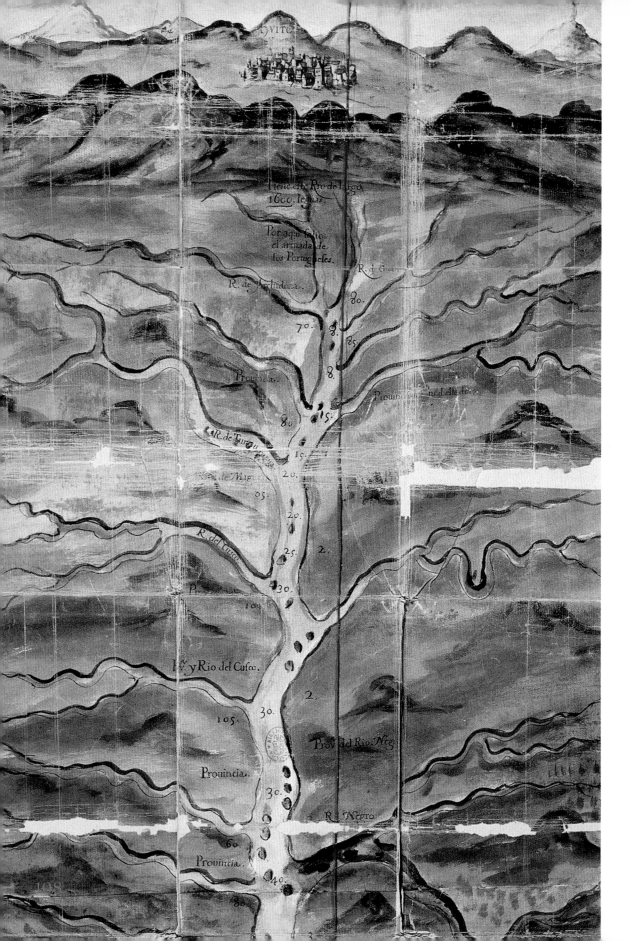

Even if we are still far from recording the position of every lake and reef, the depth of every abyss and the direction and volume of every expanse of water, there has been no shortage of attempts to do so. In *Geography*, Ptolemy tries to reproduce the course of the Nile, but the lack of data prevents him from locating the source. Instead, he chose to have the river start in the mountains on the moon.

Later, Westerners set out around the world and noticed, by collaborating with the aboriginal populations of North America, that the waterways on the maps that the Native Americans had helped prepare had the same status as the land routes. The Natives had treated all means of transportation in the same way, which had led to many errors in interpretation.

South America:
The Amazon River. (National
Library of Spain, Madrid.)

It was not until the arrival of the Reverend Pierre Desceliers (1500–1558) — a cartographer from Dieppe who initiated numerous overseas expeditions, particularly to New York Bay, Newfoundland and Indonesia — that hydrography was considered a true discipline. Desceliers gathered information from travelers upon their return and specialized in drawing nautical charts and coastlines.

Through Desceliers's work, Dieppe became the first French port where one could learn the nautical sciences based on rules and principles, and the first nautical theories began to be developed in Upper Normandy. Captains, pilots who no longer sailed and clerics taught the practical and theoretical rudiments. Cartographers also tried to gather all the information essential to navigation: calculating the tides, latitude, magnetic variation and the like.

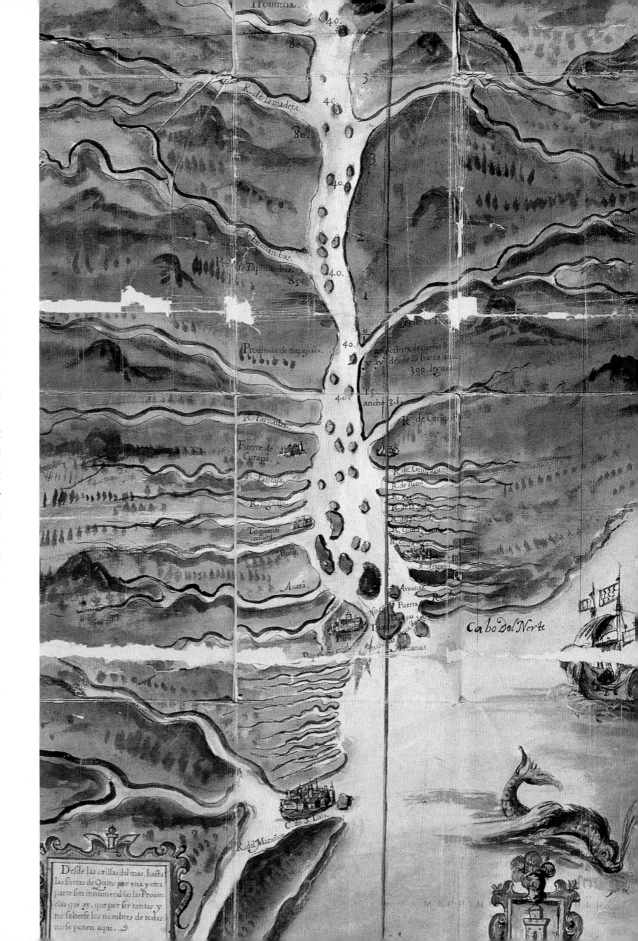

Foreign Seas

Polynesians relied on the motion of the sea on rocks to travel on the open water around their islands. They also used navigational charts made from sticks and shells to help them establish markers. In the West, the Mediterranean, known as *mare nostrum* (Latin for "our sea"), was the absolute point of reference. The horizon lay beyond its basin. The ocean assumed another name and became for some "the Great Sea."

In the 12th century, the grammarian and philosopher Guillaume de Conches spoke of the "True Sea" on a diagram representing how water flows. On this diagram waves arrive from the east or west and set off to the north or south. Those who sailed along the Mediterranean coast under a clear and starry sky had no need to be great navigators, and the use of very detailed maps did not seem to be essential to have a successful trip. It took the crossing of oceans for navigational tools worthy of the name to finally be developed. It also took men who dared to confront the sea despite their fears of its waves, storms and tides.

Ships, solid caravels, compasses, quadrants, astrolabes and sand glasses for marking time — sailors who ventured beyond the Mediterranean on long journeys had to equip themselves

differently if they did not want to end up like frogs around a pond, an expression coined at the time to refer to Mediterranean navigators. The first navigational charts were called pilot books. They indicated the routes to follow along the coasts. The reference points — capes, ports, river mouths, rivers — were only crudely drawn because cartographers knew they could always be seen from the sea.

Christopher Columbus said that during his first voyage, his sailors started to cry when leaving the Canary Islands because as they lost sight of the last piece of land, they believed that they would never again see anything remotely resembling a continent. Their imaginations took off. Until then, the suppliers of globes and maps had showed landmasses surrounded by vast, intractable blocks of ocean. The inhabited world appeared like a large island lost in the middle of a sea that was populated by monsters, boiled at the equator and turned any living soul into a block of ice at the poles.

"Haaven-Kaart, Middellandse-Zee en Archipelago"
(map of ports, the Mediterranean and the archipelago)
from Le Gran et nouveau atlas de la marine
hydrographique dans lequel est compris &
demonstré toutes les côtes du monde connu (Big
and new atlas of marine hydrography in which all the
coasts of the known world are included and shown) by
Johannes Van Keulen and published in Amsterdam.
(1715. Municipal Library, Versailles, France.)

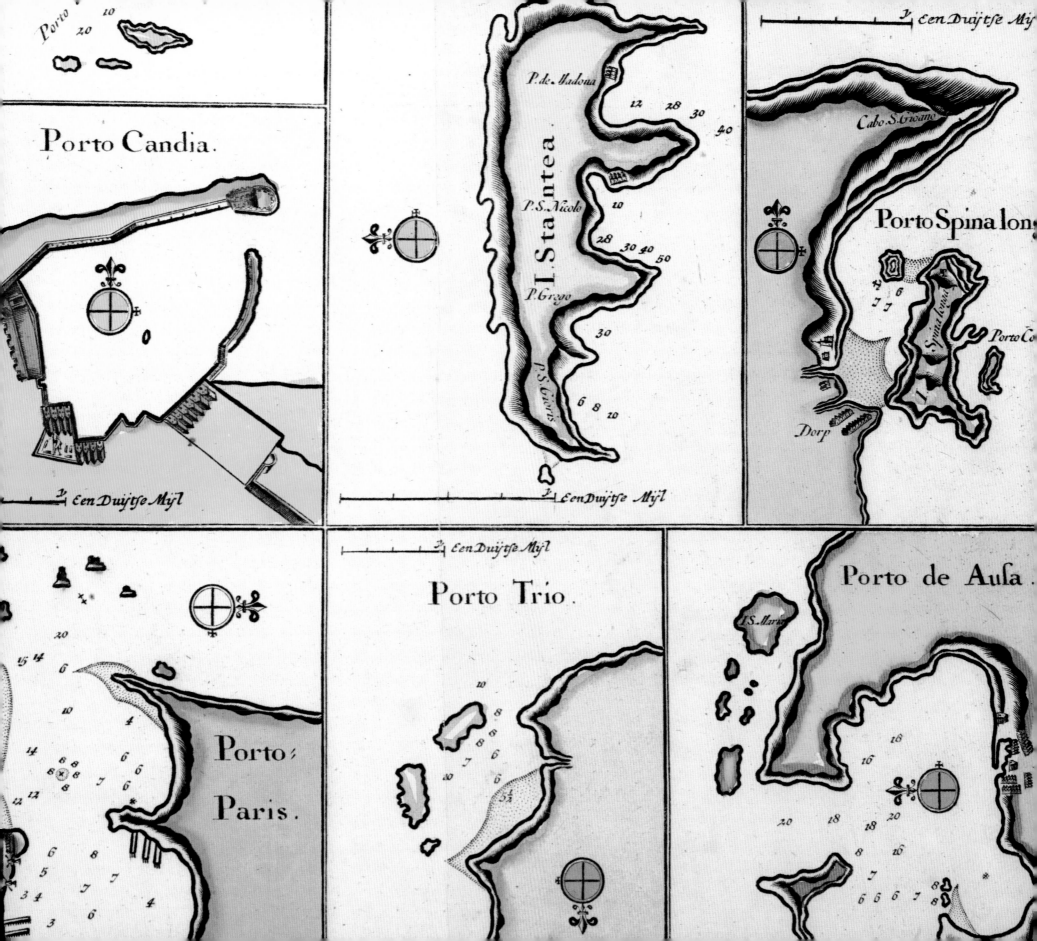

Porto Candia.

Een Duijtse Mijl

P. de Madona

P. S. Nicolo

I. Sta ntea .

P. Grego

P. S. Croris

Een Duijtse Mijl

Cabo S. Groano

Porto Spina long

Spina longa

Porto Co

Dorp

Een Duijtse Mijl

Porto Trio.

Porto Paris.

Porto de Aula.

I. S. Marm

Mocha

Perim Island

Strait of Bab out Mandeb

Chotea

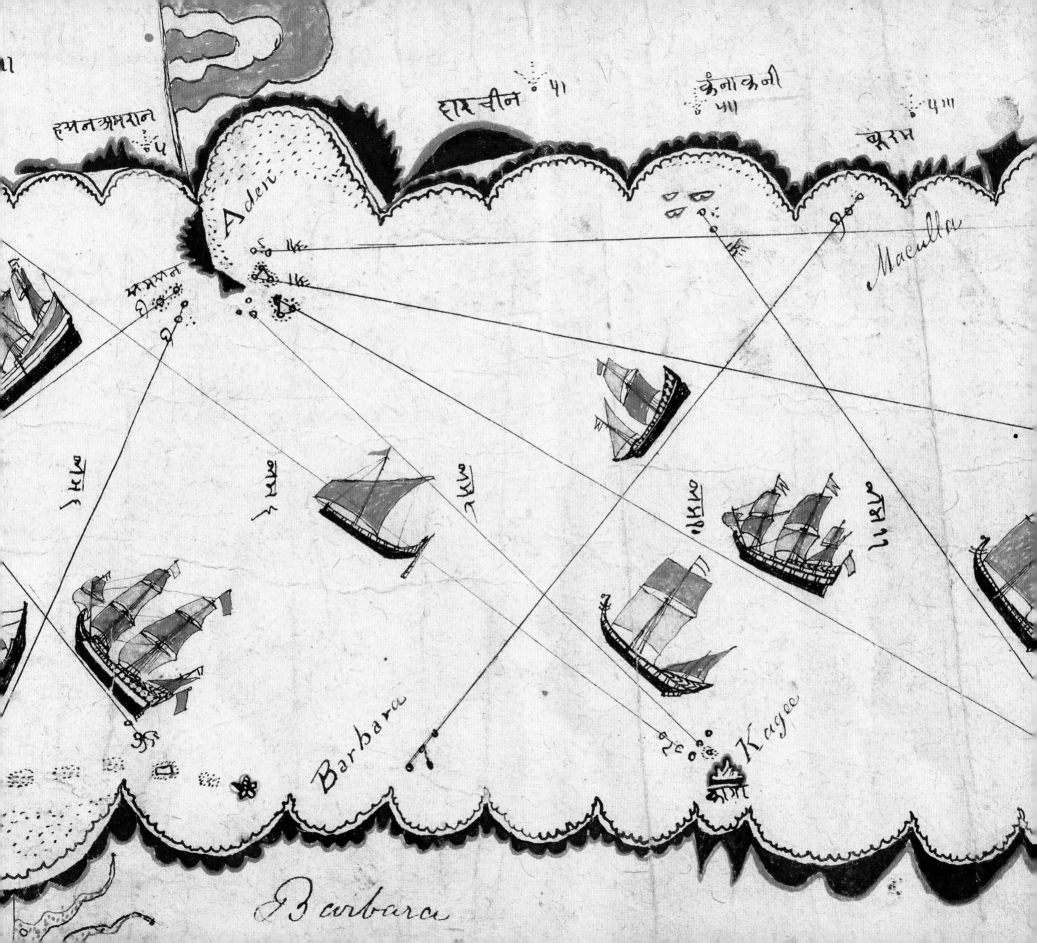

Т he appearance of portolan charts indicates a geographical turning point and demonstrates that a new vision of the world and, in particular, the sea was starting to take hold. The 32 rhumb lines that corresponded to the angles of routes gave structure to maps. Inspired by Ptolemy's mathematical projections, the sea was "rationalized," and sea trade prompted the rise of new maps. During a voyage to Tunisia in 1270, Saint Louis took a map with him, and the King of Aragon required every ship on his expeditions to carry two maps beginning in 1354. Then the portolans changed, and the use of refined parchment leads one to believe that very few of these charts were actually used on the sea. Instead, they became luxury goods used by wealthy shipowners and merchants. The Majorcan portolans of the 14th and 15th centuries had sumptuous illustrations and added descriptions of the coasts, rivers and territories to the descriptions of the sea. Each owner could thereby see the extent of his wealth from his palace.

PRECEDING DOUBLE PAGE: *Red Sea: Nautical chart of the Gulf of Aden and the Red Sea. (Circa 1810. Royal Geographical Society, London, England.)*

OPPOSITE: *Amazonia, Brazil: Detail of a map of America from a copy of* Atlas maior (Major atlas) *by Joan Blaeu. (1686. Prins Hendrik Martime Museum, Rotterdam, The Netherlands.)*

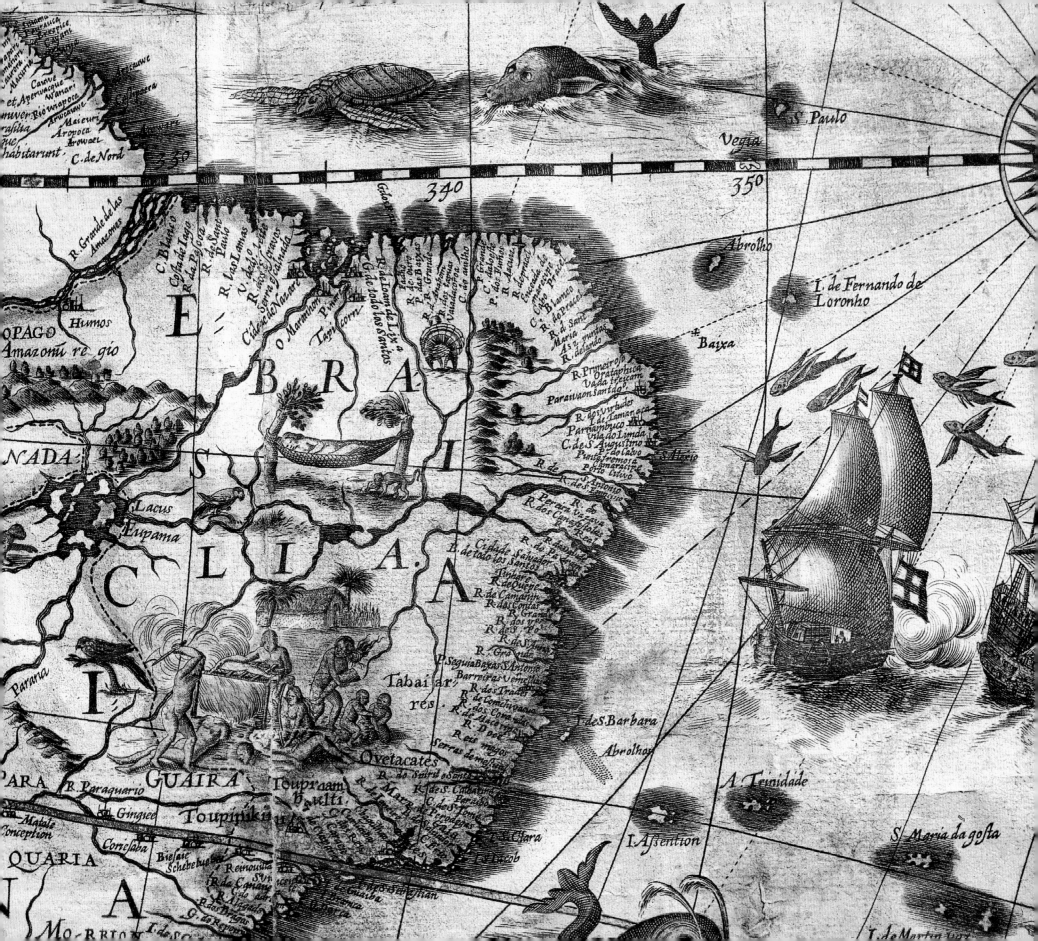

A few centuries later in Nagasaki, among other cities, nautical cartography became highly accurate, describing islands, ports, inland cities, distances and a precise plan of the city of Edo. It is said that the 17th century was the golden age of Japanese cartography. The civil war had ended years earlier and business was thriving, so merchants ordered maps. These maps were enormous and richly decorated. Lines were created using Indian ink and enhanced with gold and silver powder. Some maps detailed monuments or surprising places. Many passages used by ships reflected the intensity of the traffic and economic wealth. Maps showing land and sea routes were the most prized. Gold and diamond mines, silk routes and salt caravans — the conquest of the sea and the continents no longer instilled fear but rather dreaming. From that moment on, the seas were tamed.

Japan: A section of a map of land and sea routes from Edo to Nagasaki that shows the Shikoku-Kobe Bay of Osaka. (17th century. National Library of France, Paris.)

Personal Projections

Order and Disorder

"We called them 'voyageurs'
Those people who opened up
the vast expanse of the Canadian West.
I felt what they experienced. For less.
Thanks Air Canada."

Jean-Didier Urbain, *L'Idiot du voyage: Histoires de touristes*

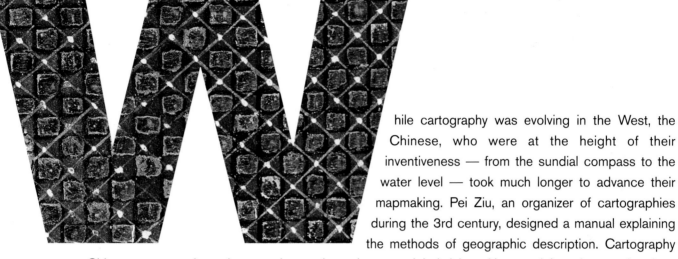

hile cartography was evolving in the West, the Chinese, who were at the height of their inventiveness — from the sundial compass to the water level — took much longer to advance their mapmaking. Pei Ziu, an organizer of cartographies during the 3rd century, designed a manual explaining the methods of geographic description. Cartography gave China, a country of travelers, warriors and merchants, a global vision of its people's various explorations and reassured them that they were indeed the "middle kingdom," the English translation of the country's Mandarin name.

Therefore, the Chinese were extremely exasperated when they discovered, much later, that they had been relegated to the right edge of a map prepared by the Jesuits. Diplomats in the West sensed the approaching incident, and Father Matteo Ricci, responsible for presenting a new planisphere to the Chinese, corrected the order of the world: the celestial empire was instead placed in the center. In the end, these two cartographic powers agreed on a vision of the world that suited them. Thus, Africa and America were shown here and there as vague islands, as small points lost in the middle of the ocean.

However, empires, too, come and go. Eastern Africa became German, the French established themselves in Indochina and the Commonwealth embraced the world. A map reflects the era in which it is drawn, embodying the stakes and the conflicts. They also reflect an era's illusions, as shown by a map of Honduras produced in 1891. The country was semiarid at the time but, magnified by the cartographer F. Bianconi, it appears in full bloom with lines indicating railway tracks that cross the country, with the note "under construction." Over 100 years later, the train is still not running. Therefore, one has to be careful when using a map's key. Today, planispheres of Israel, the Palestine Territories, Pakistan and India, in particular, will vary according to the nationality of the cartographer. Every country will also always be Longitude Zero, the point at which east and west begin, to its inhabitants.

Battle Plans

When the Ottoman Empire — or the Sublime Porte, as it was called in reference to the monumental entrance of the Grand Vizier of Istanbul — established the maps of its territories in the 16th century, the cartographer spread Persian characters out over the conquered lands. There were no longer countries or borders, just a continuous strip of land that highlighted the victories of the Turkish state since the 11th century: Anatolia, the region around the Black Sea, Syria, Palestine, Mesopotamia, the Arabian Peninsula and North Africa.

However, the control of trade on the Mediterranean remained outside the grasp of the Ottomans. To gain it, Suleiman the Magnificent built a military fleet. And yet it did not matter that the caravels, their sails unfurled, were shown proudly sailing along the coast as far as Spain in atlases, the fate of the empire did not change. In 1571, it had to give up its insatiable expansion, beaten by the Spanish and Venetian navies at Lepanto. This battle is considered the pinnacle of naval strategy. For the first time, ships were armed with cannons and maneuvered to board the galleys. The human toll was also great, with more than 30,000 Turkish lives lost.

Map of the Crusades based on an Ottoman manuscript. (17th century. Istanbul University Library, Turkey.)

6½ Vaam
6½ Brasses

Fort St. Louis
20. C.

D

D

D

D

Infirmerie

B

B

B

Madrague ou Pêche du Ton

F

F

F

Cap de Toulon

Ste Marguerite

Fort Ste Marguerite

C

D

D

Riviere de

Hollandse Schepen

Hollandse Schepen

Engelse Schepen

RANÉE

Armée navale des Alliez

However, it was not only on the ground that military intelligence needed to be demonstrated. Arms of persuasion, maps were also part of a country's arsenal. The enemy would only have to look at the ships on Van Keulen's atlas of the siege of Toulon to tremble with fear. Not only is the battle plan perfect on paper, with properly aligned ships preventing any escape by the enemy, but the cannons bombarding the targets on land never seem to miss. A thin and uninterrupted line shows each cannonball unmistakably reaching its goal. On maps, war seemed clean and surgical. Colored flags were planted on territories that were to be conquered or that had been annexed. Land could be drawn and parceled up far from the violence of battle.

Fort St. Louis
20. C.

Toulon Harbor: The city and harbor of Toulon with its forts and the naval forces of the Allies. The letter D corresponds to the galliots to be bombed. From Le gran et nouveau atlas de la marine hydrographique dans lequel est compris & demonstré toutes les côtes du monde connu *(Big and new atlas of marine hydrography in which all the coasts of the known world are included and shown) by Johannes Van Keulen, published in Amsterdam. (1715. Municipal Library, Versailles, France.)*

It was in the 17th century that the first proper attempts at military cartography were made. Prior to that, the usual tradespeople made military maps: "painters, notchers, embroiderers, glassmakers and illuminators," explains historian Monique Pelletier in her book on French cartography during the Renaissance. They made a few sketches of the fortress and the construction of the ramparts, or they made discrete observations on the subject of neighboring fortresses. Over time, cartographers moved from such maps to detailed plans with highly accurate topographical descriptions. In the 16th century, the Italian mapmakers were sought after for their knowledge and ability. Kings ordered plans that became renowned for their precision and constant proportions. The interest in military maps grew, and states began to depend more and more on espionage. Thus, when offered a map of England by a Flemish painter, King Francis I of France warmly welcomed him, his wife and his children. Elsewhere, an Italian technician studied the fortifications on the upper Somme, and on the other side of the border, the Spanish hired a Flemish engineer.

Island of Saint Jago, Cape Verde: Attack by Francis Drake commanding the Elizabeth Bonaventure, *November 17, 1585. Today the island is more commonly called Santiago. (The British Library, London.)*

Hoobe Churche

Hoobe village

the towne of brichampton

Upon this rocke may lond & ordinance vnladed by any nation than

a fole in the mydell of the towne

the towne fyre the towne cage

Here landed the Gale

Shippes may ride all somer nere to a myle the towne in v fathome water.

These grete shippes ride at hazard vode there by shoting into the hille valeis to they so fore oppresse the towne that the Countrey dare not adventure to

Under Louis XIV, maps became even more detailed. Relief appeared, and, soon after, the city plan could be accurately reproduced in the form of a model. The city's faults were studied in minute detail by Vauban (1633–1707), the Marshall of France, who suggested to the king the addition of new strategic intersections. Victorious at the sieges of Tournai, Douai and Lille, Vauban earned the title of Commissioner General of Fortifications. He then allied new ways of attacking, such as ricochet firing, the use of grenades and the bayonet for the infantry, to cartography. This is how he successfully led more than 53 sieges and built nearly 300 strongholds.

Studying the land in a form that allowed it to be modeled, transformed or reconfigured as one pleased proved to be of great use when assessing military maneuvers. History is arranged in atlases according to the battles.

England: A map drawn between 1539 and 1545 that shows the 1514 attack on Brighton by French ships. (The British Library, London.)

Organizing the Resistance

No matter how often neighboring fortresses might have been spied on, attacking was one thing, and defending was another. Louis XIV had an atlas of strongholds made to complement his relief maps. Cartographers also prepared a richly illustrated copy that related to his campaigns in his honor. In the 18th century, the East India Company, proud of England's territorial conquests, felt the need to accurately map the Indian continent. They not only sought to find out its potential but also to protect company trading posts. James Rennel is renown for having been the general surveyor of Bengal from 1767 to 1777, and he is known as the man behind Indian geography. In 1765, he began to map the eastern region of the Indian subcontinent. His surveys were sent to England and distributed to a large public, who were excited by the idea of discovering distant countries of the British Empire.

Arabian Peninsula: Portuguese fort
with merchants on the Arabian coasts.
(Private collection.)

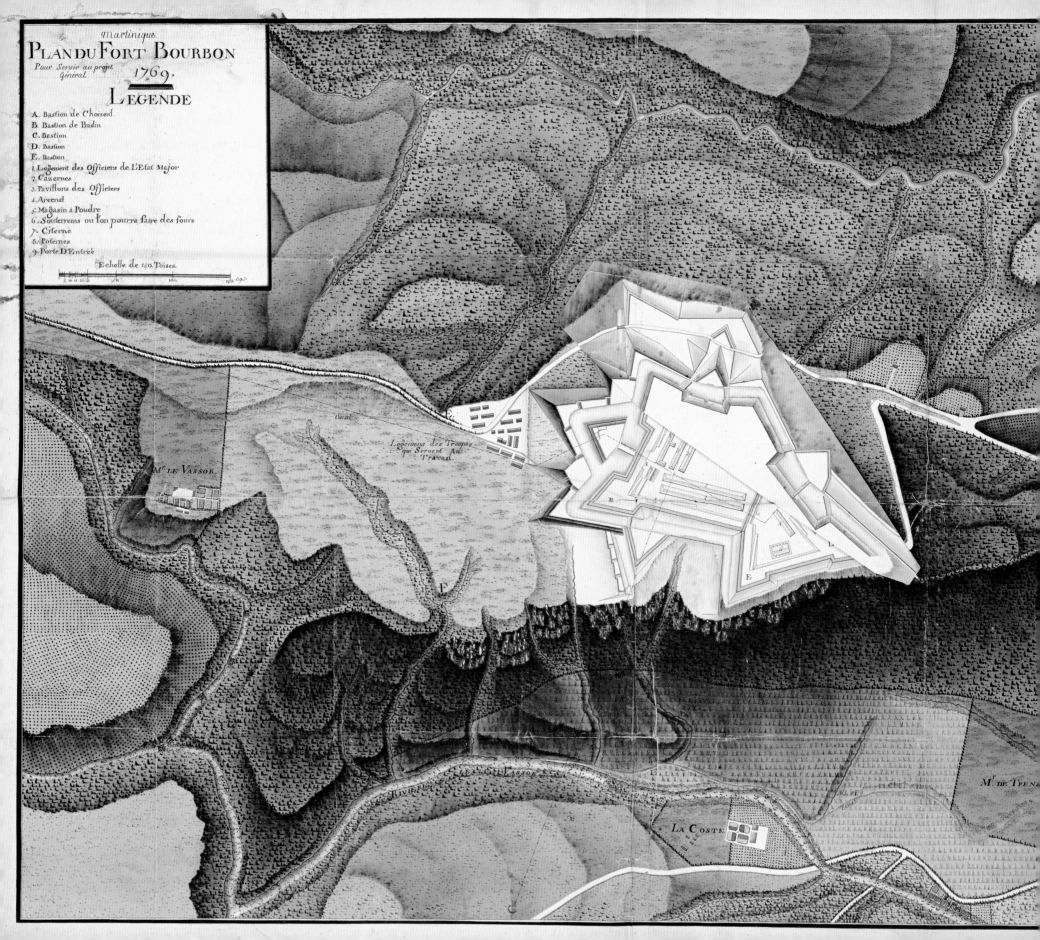

Martinique.
PLAN DU FORT BOURBON
Pour Servir au projet Général **1769.**
LEGENDE

A. Bastion de Choiseul.
B. Bastion de Baslin.
C. Bastion.
D. Bastion.
E. Bastion.
1. Logement des Officiers de L'Etat Major.
2. Cazernes.
3. Pavillons des Officiers.
4. Arcenal.
5. Magasin à Poudre.
6. Souterrems ou l'on pourra faire des fours.
7. Citerne.
8. Poternes.
9. Porte D'Entrée.

Echelle de 150. Toises.

Mⁿ LE VASSOR.

Canal.

Logemens des Troupes qui Servent au Travail.

RAVINE.

RIVIÈRE

M. DE TREN

LA COSTE

Mᵉ VASSOR

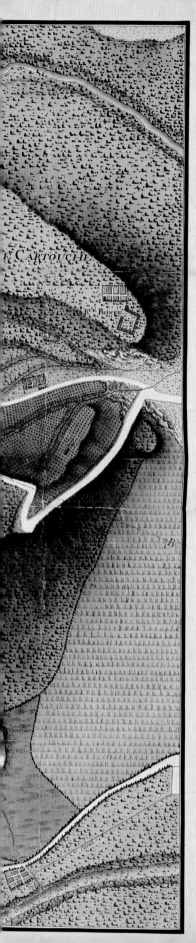

E CARTOUCHE

RTE RUINÉE

B

The plan of Fort William in Calcutta, with its irregular octagonal shape punctuated by seven gates, bears witness to this fort's impenetrable character. Fort William was built in 1781 after the ancient citadel was taken in an attack by a local nabob, Siraj-ud-daula, who sacked the city. The different incidents that pitted them against the colonial powers, including the French, also led the English to increase Calcutta's fortifications. It must be said that Calcutta, at that time and until 1911, was the capital of the raj and a highly strategic location in the organization of the British Empire. Built on the site of an ancient village, the new fort was surrounded by an enormous field, the Maidan, which itself was crossed by canals that could be flooded it in the event of an attack. The fort could also shelter 10,000 soldiers. Was its imposing mass enough to dissuade any rebels? In any event, the English did not hesitate to widely distribute its image, which they believe would act as a warning.

OPPOSITE PAGE: *Martinique: Plan of Fort Bourbon. (1769. With the kind permission of the National Geographic Institute.)*

ABOVE: *India:. Fort William in Calcutta, Bengal. (The British Library, London.)*

W here to set up camp, where to rest and the
possible speed of travel — military maps provided a wealth of information and
grew in scope over time. They were drawn on a large scale and updated based on
army advances. While some maps remained secret for strategic reasons, others were
used to help shape public opinion. In the 19th century, newspaper readers were used to seeing
military maps. Their sponsors understood that, just like patriotic songs, maps could be used to
reinvigorate the troops and, along with them, public opinion. The maps served as propaganda. Political
manipulators are masters in the art of making maps lie. Mark Monmonier, a professor of American geography,
recorded such abuses of cartography in his book *How to Lie with Maps*. Maps, he explained, impose an image
of authority. Unsuspecting people do not see the ideology hidden in them because maps are first and
foremost considered "real." The artisans of persuasion know perfectly well what codes are in effect and
what can touch their audience: national pride, territorial conquest, achievable targets. They will truncate
scales or outrageously enlarge some topographical signs and symbols; as for the colors they select,
these can arouse the strongest emotions. The religious wars of the 17th century, Nazi
propaganda and the Cold War of the 20th century remain the most striking examples of these
cartographical distortions and abuses. It is always important to know how to look at
whatever fiction is at work behind a map.

*Naval war between the German
and English navies in 1941, taken
from the German magazine
Signal. (Private collection.)*

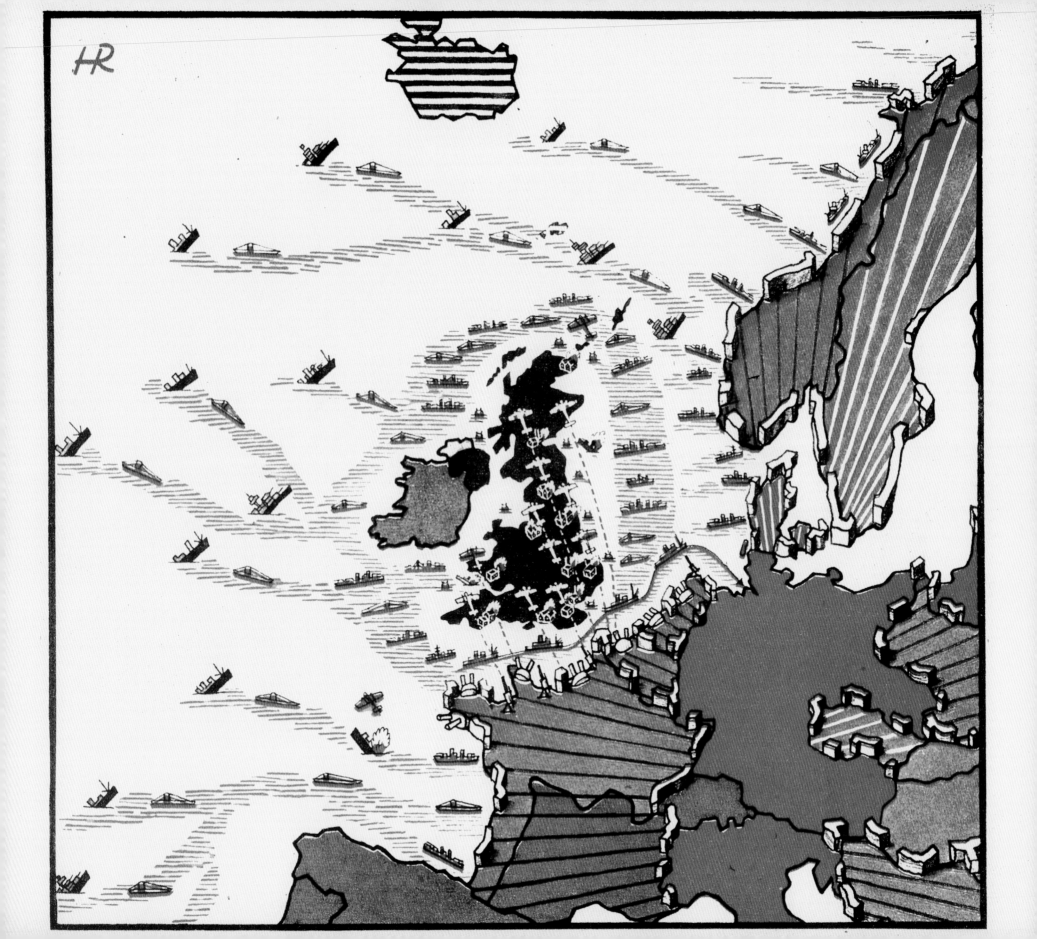

Signification of these markes,
To the crosses hath bin. discouere
what beyond is by relation
Kings howses 2
Ordinary howses 2

Power of Persuasion

Virginia, United States: Map of the English colony from the expeditions of Secretary of State William Strachey. (17th century. The British Library, London.)

"From the mouth of the James River, over the hills and the adjoining rich valleys, enhanced by beneficial streams that must necessarily discharge into the peaceful Indian sea": such were the comments that accompanied a map of Virginia from 1651. The creation of the city of Jamestown in 1607 marked the beginning of British settlement in North America. The first emigrants were, in fact, men persecuted in England for their religious or political beliefs. They were designated "English separatists" belonging to a dissident sect of the Anglican Church. What future settler would not be seduced by this idyllic vision of the New World?

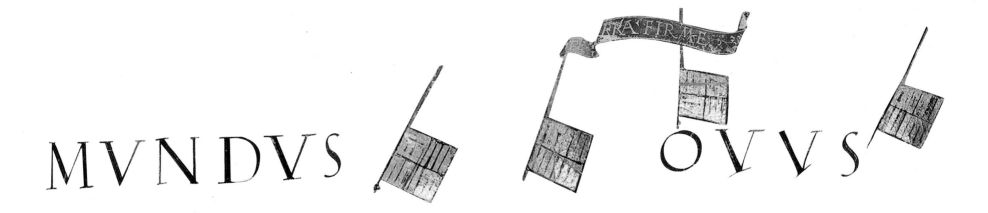

MVNDVS OVVS

Just like well-chosen adjectives and other vocabulary, maps of new colonies were deliberately positive to attract settlers. The coasts often seemed less jagged, and the passages and links appeared easy. Moreover, nature was pacified; the mountains were round, and the landscapes were highlighted in a pretty, springlike green. As for the people, they do not appear on the maps. If ever a few natives are shown, they generally appear to be benevolent. Kneeling before the newcomers, their arms are sometimes covered in offerings, like the Indian brahman who piously offers the sacred texts to "Brittania," an allegory of the British Empire. This gesture had the same value as a title being conferred. Often lacking information, cartographers wanted to fill the map with attractive elements. Whatever the cost, maps had to advertise new conquests, and, thanks to a whole series of ornaments (title boxes, vignettes, wind roses, borders), they loaded geography with eminently political messages. Monumental arcs, royal emblems, escutcheons and knights brandishing swords all reinforced a map's power of persuasion.

Atlantic Ocean: A detail from the Atlas Miller by Lopo Homem that shows slaves from Africa and the West Indies. (1519. National Library of France, Paris.)

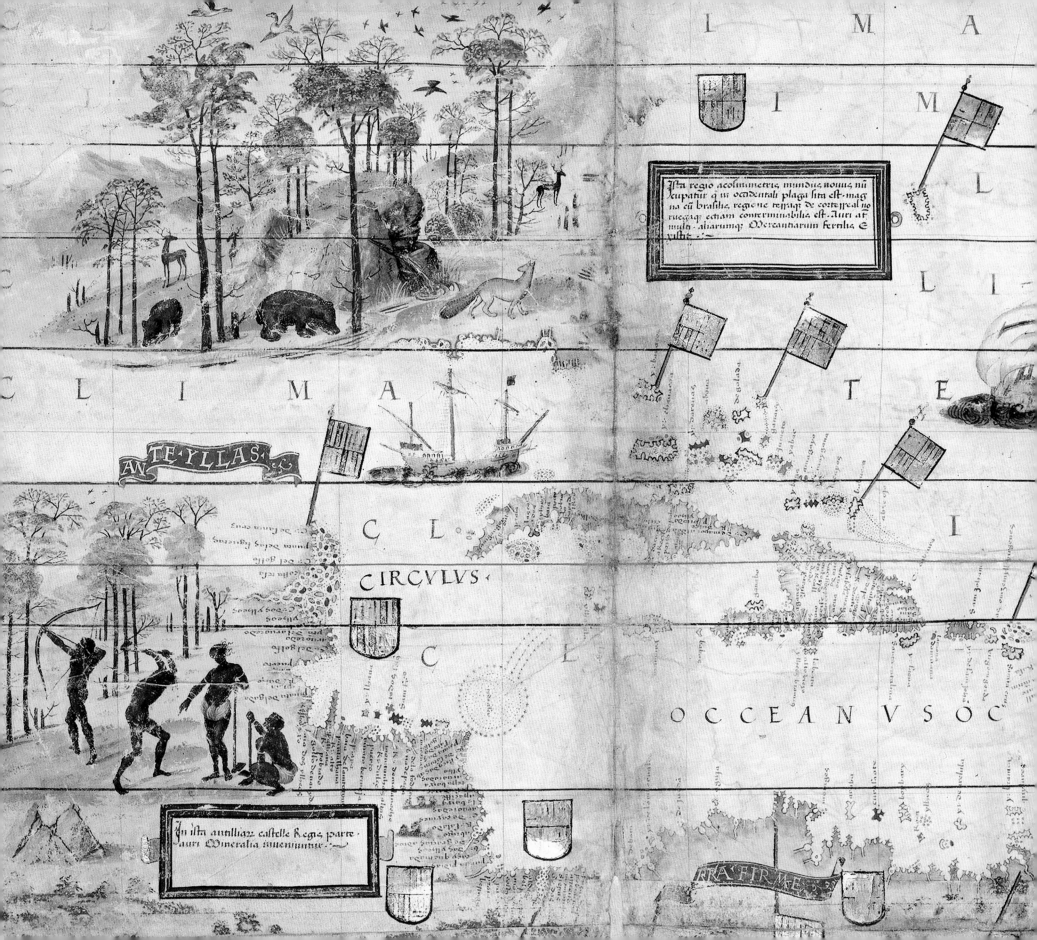

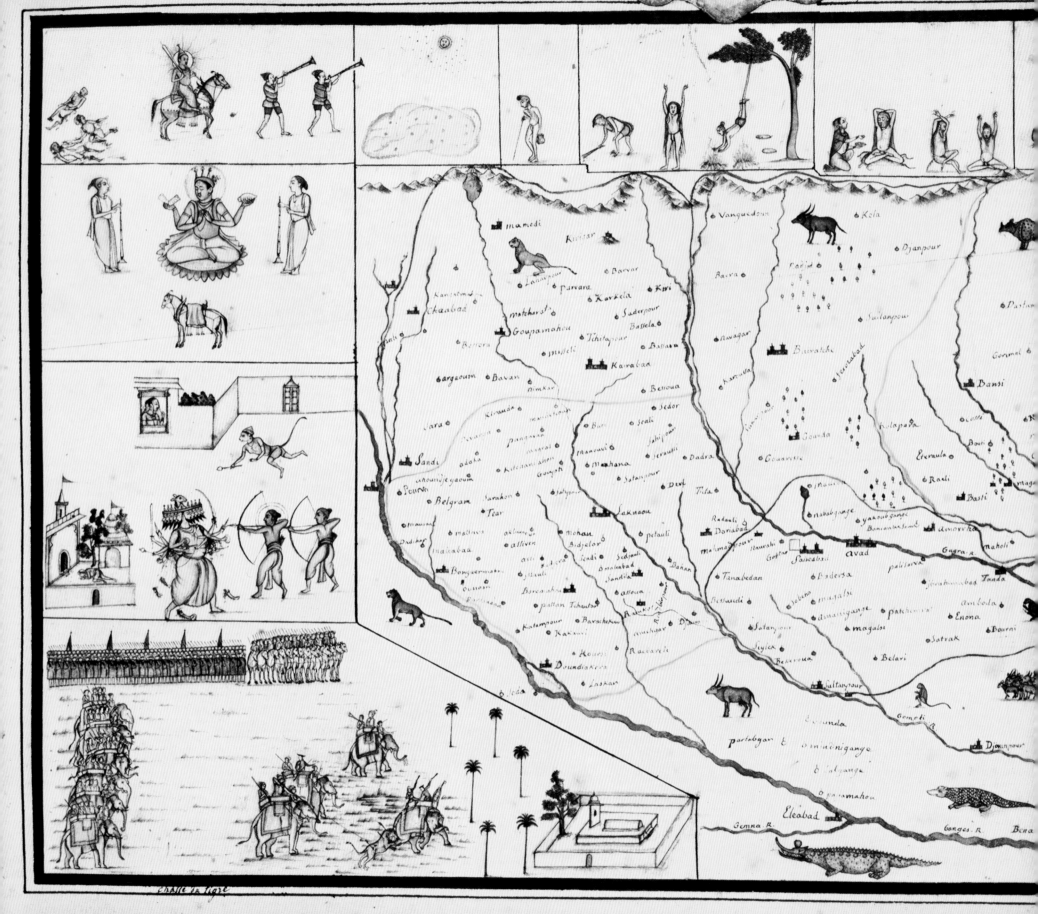

Vanquedeun · Kola

· mamedi

Kussar

· Djanpour

· Barvar

Baira

· Lanapour · parvara

· Karkela · Kwi

Kangoloudou

Chaabad · matcharst

Awagar

· Baurotche

Goupamahou · Tchapour · Basela

· Bettera · miseli

Karnala

Ferozabad

· Bansi

· Karaban

· Bejoua

· Bavan

· Gormal

sargooum

· Djankar

Goanda

Kirunda

· Jedor

· Goanriste

· Kolapada

· Eteraula

Sara

Bari · Seali

· Rasti

odaha pangavan miras Jahijour

Sandi

kitchanahou · mahana · Ferauti Dadra

· Basti

Belgram Saruhon · Tear · Satanpour · Devi Tila · nababganga

Poura

· Amorto

· Naholi

· mohau · Laknaou Radaali · yasoubgange

mattura alliven Doriabad Baniantasend

· Bidjelor petauti mahmadpour Naurshi Gostu · Avad Gugra R.

Bonguernasi · Jendi · Sedjauti Sancabad · palsara

· Tanabedan · Badersa · Tanda

pattan Tchautar Santila Bettandi Sohna · imagalsi · Ambola

Katampour · atteoa Satanpour Amaniganga · patchaura · Enona

Barachekei Seylea · magalsi · Belari · Bourni

Kouri · Rawarela Bebeoua · Satrak

Doundiakera Sultanpour

· Laskan · Gomoti

partabgan · komeda

· Jedo · imaunigange

· Salganga

· payamahou

· Eleabad

Jemna R. Ganges R. Bena

· Djanpour

After the great discoveries, European expansion only advanced overseas. In the 19th century, with the help of the industrial revolution and demographic growth, states sought to increase their sovereignty outside their borders. Whether they were strictly motivated by economics — such as securing new wealth and raw materials in Southern Asia, Africa and Latin America — or trying to find new opportunities for their excess production, as in India, or searching for a settlement colony such as North America, Siberia or Australia, cartography reassured European nations of the merits of their enterprise. It especially supported them by defining and limiting their territory.

Moghul Empire: The fauna, flora and gods of India. (1770. The British Library, London.)

One of the most symbolic examples of colonial maps remains the map of North America with its provinces drawn using a string. It aptly demonstrates how little importance was attached to the national identities of the native populations. Each country produced maps, and each one used its own data. It did not matter if the real extent of the territory was not known, as demonstrated on a map commissioned by King Charles II of England. In 1778, as settlement in North America developed, the need arose to create a precise grid of the region, and a geographer-surveyor was duly mandated to do it. Numerous legal disputes were born these approximations. States had to regularly send their experts to correct the "dangerous" maps of their neighbors, who were quick to nibble away at, or even annex, new concessions. Thus, Joseph Bernard, Marquis de Chabert, landed in Canada in 1750 by order of the king of France to scrupulously record all the territory that belonged to the English and to the French. Until the conflicts stabilized, North America saw the production of all types of maps, on which borders changed based on the desires of the interested parties.

Martinique: From Le gran et nouveau atlas de la marine hydrologique dans lequel est compris & demonstré toutes les côtes du monde connu *(Big and new atlas of marine hydrography in which all the coasts of the known world are included and shown) by Johannes Van Keulen, published in Amsterdam. (1715. Municipal library, Versailles, France.)*

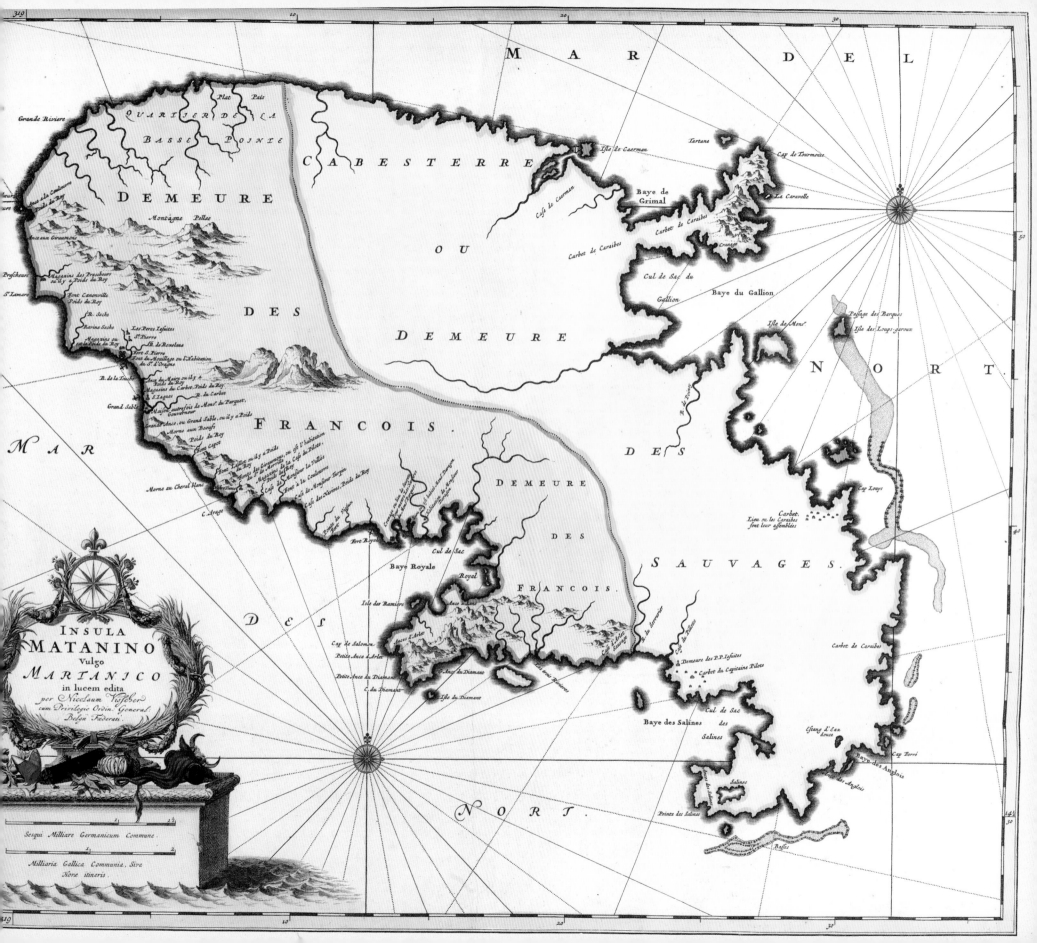

MAR   DEL

CABESTERRE

Plat Pais

QUARTIER DE LA

BASSE POINTE

Grande Riviere

DEMEURE

Montagne Pelée

Anse à la Couleuvre
Poids du Roy

Prescheurs
S.t Lamare

Magazins des Prescheurs
ou il y a Poids du Roy

Font Canonville
Poids du Roy

B. Seche

Ravine Seche

Magazins ou
est le Poids du Roy

Les Peres Iesuites
S.t Pierre

Fh. le Roselme

Fort S. Pierre

Font du Mouillage ou l'Habitation
du S.t d'Oragne

B. de la Touche

Anse à Maire ou il y a
Poids du Roy

Magazins du Carbet, Poids du Roy

B. de S. Iagues

R. du Carbet

Grand Sable

Maison autrefois de Mons.t du Parquet,
Gouverneur

Grande Ance, ou Grand Sable, ou il y a Poids

Morne aux Boeufs

Poids du Roy

Font Capot

Font Lasteg ou il y a Poids
du Roy

Temps des Gouyaumes, ou est l'Habitation
du de Merveille

Magazins de la Cafe du Pilote.

Morne au Cheval blanc

Magazins du Chey
Poids du Roy

Cafe de Monsieur la Vallie

Font à la Couleuvre

Cafe de Monsieur Iurgin

Cafe des Navires, Poids du Roy

C. Arago

DES

DEMEURE

OU

DEMEURE

Cafe de Caerman

Isle de Caerman

Baye de
Grimal

Carbet de Caraibes

Carbet de Caraibes

Tartane

Cap de Tourmente

La Caravelle

Cranage

Cul de Sac du

Gallion

Baye du Gallion

Isle de Mons.t

Passage des Barques

Isle des Loups-garoux

R. du Roceli

NORT

FRANCOIS.

FRANCOIS.

DEMEURE

DES

SAUVAGES.

DES

MAR

NORT.

Fort Royal

Cul de Sac

Royal

Baye Royale

Isle des Ramiers

Cap de Salomon

Ances d'Arlet

Petite Ance d'Arlet

Petite Ance du Diamant

C. du Diamant

Ance à Latte

Ance du Diamant

Isle du Diamant

Les trois Rivieres

Cap Salvage

R. du Simarin

Cafe du Blancs

Demeure des P.P. Iesuites

Carbet du Capitaine Pilote

Cul de Sac
des Salines

Baye des Salines

des

Salines

Pointe des Salines

Salines

Bassos

Lieu ou les Caraibes
font leur assemblées

Carbet.

Cap Loups

Carbet de Caraibes

Estang d'Eau
douce

Baye des Anglois

Cap Ferré

Ance des Anglois

INSULA
MATANINO
Vulgo
MARTANICO
in lucem edita
per Nicolaum Visscher
cum Privilegio Ordin. General.
Belgii Faederati.

Sesqui Milliare Germanicum Commune.

Milliaria Gallica Communia, Sive
Nore itineris.

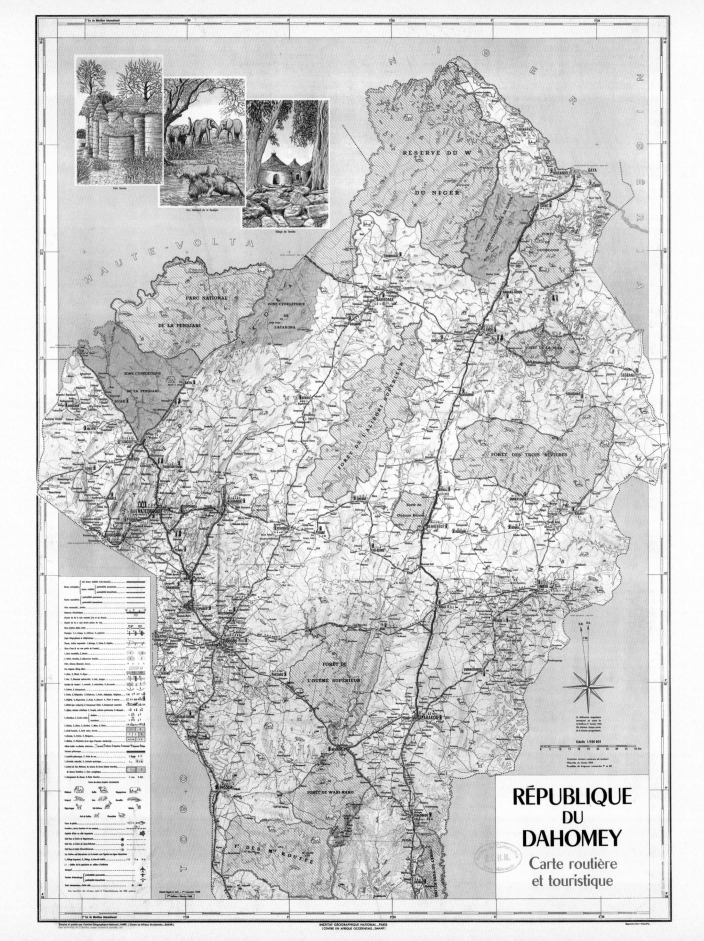

RÉPUBLIQUE DU DAHOMEY

Carte routière et touristique

During this time, on the other side of the globe in Africa, navigators and explorers were also advancing, convinced, as the first pages of many atlases show, that the world was already theirs. They wanted to be seen, to be drawn on the frontispiece of an atlas with their compass and sextant in hand and with the air of a conqueror even before they had discovered any "unknown lands."

It is easy to understand which ideology motivated the empires and how the system of colonization was being set up. It is enough to look closely at the details that decorate maps. From the 16th to the 19th centuries, there was a great constant in the way in which the "other" — the strange lands — were re-presented. African men were shown striking poses more worthy of Antiquity, and their features were astonishingly similar to those of Europeans. There were no longer any chiefs but rather kings, signifying that the political system must be the same. In short, the atlases seem to indicate that everything would be for the better in the best of all worlds but for a few aboriginals riding exotic animals in the corners. The prejudices were hidden in the borders of the maps.

Republic of Dahomey: Road and tourism map of what is present-day Benin. (Circa 1960. With the kind permission of the National Geographic Institute.)

Point of View

The Chinese named their country in different ways. The word *Guo* means nation. In calligraphy, it is represented by a territory defended by a wall and weapons. But the most current term today is *Zhongguó. Zhong* means center, axis, middle or intermediary. The design of its calligraphic symbol is a line crossing through the middle of a square. Therefore, it is not surprising that the "Middle Kingdom" has had an ethnocentric vision of the world since Antiquity. But it is not alone — all states like to give themselves the starring role. Moreover, who can say otherwise, given they were the first sponsors of maps? Geographic realities matter little. The main thing is to establish one's power in the eyes of the world.

But what is valid for China, whose importance is certainly undeniable, is almost as valid for Fiji, Liechtenstein or Monaco. Each one shows an unfortunate tendency to put itself in the middle of its maps. This is how planispheres impose a nation's vision, order and hierarchy.

Until the 19th century, Zhongguó meant "the center of the country" to the Chinese. The emperor was placed in the center, and the rest of the country was imagined as concentric rings moving out toward neighboring regions, referred to as "barbarian." When China opened up to the Western world, Zhongguó would come to refer to the entire country. For a long time, China would also be called the "Middle Kingdom" by the Japanese and the Koreans.

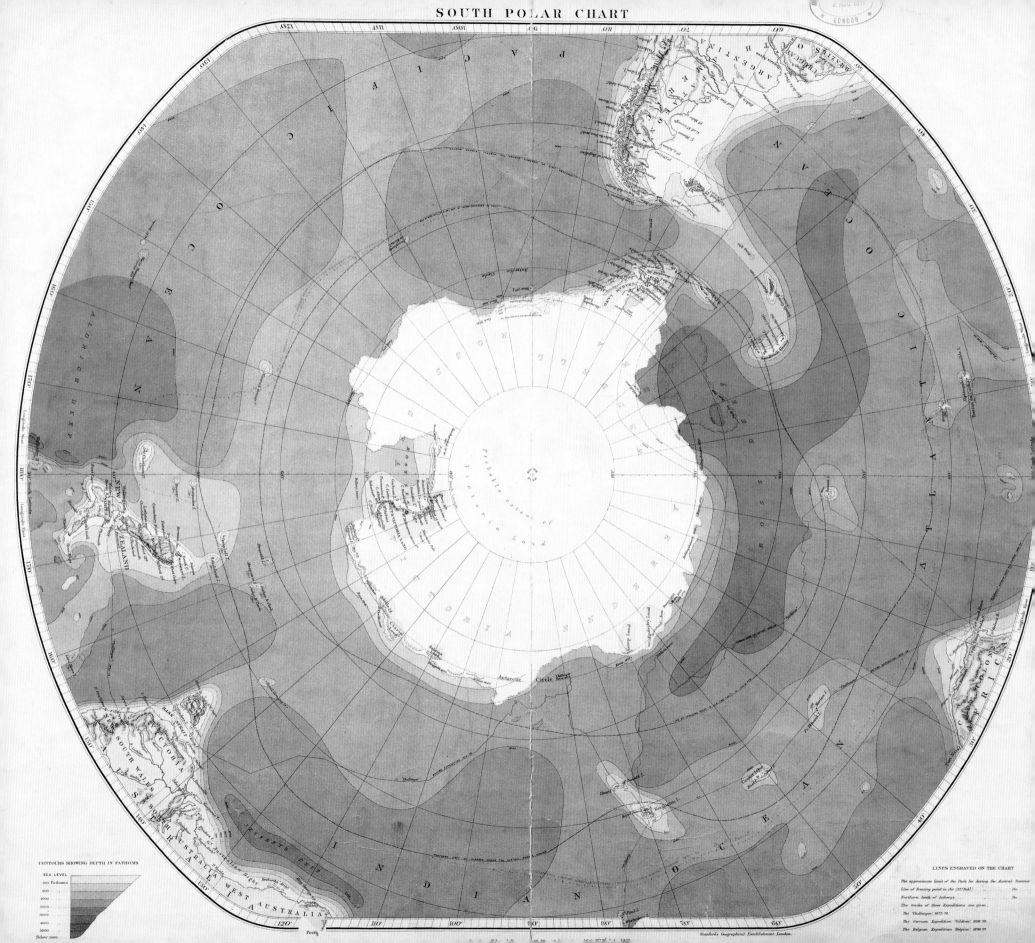

SOUTH POLAR CHART

CONTOURS SHOWING DEPTH IN FATHOMS

SEA LEVEL
100 Fathoms
500
1000
2000
3000
4000
5000
Below 5000

LINES ENGRAVED ON THE CHART

The approximate limit of the Pack Ice during the Austral Summer
Line of Freezing point in Air (32°Fah.)   Do.
Northern limit of Icebergs   Do.
The tracks of three Expeditions are given.
The 'Challenger', 1873-76.
The German Expedition 'Valdivia', 1898-99.
The Belgian Expedition 'Belgica', 1898-99.

Stanford's Geographical Establishment, London.

Historians have noticed that from the Renaissance onward, Europe and, with it, the northern hemisphere have preferred the projection introduced by Gerardus Mercator in 1569. For a long time, the system of representation perfected by this Flemish mathematician and geographer was not questioned. It was found to be the most appropriate because, with its cylindrical reproduction of the globe, it appeared to be the most accurate. Europe was unmistakably placed in the center, and its colonies were shown in miniature, which reinforced the ideological discussions of the beginning of imperial expansion during the 19th century. With this projection, the further one moves from the equator, the greater the emerging lands are distorted. For example, Africa appears much smaller. It took Arno Peters (1916–2002) to come up with a better cartographical assessment of the southern hemisphere in the 1970s. This German historian's projection shows all landmasses on the same scale. Even if the shapes are greatly changed, this vision of the world is globally more balanced. Peters also rebelled against the position of the meridian 0, referred to as the Greenwich meridian, which was established by the English during the colonial era.

South Pole: Exploration routes.
(20th century. Royal Geographical
Society. London. England.)

In addition to Peters, other geographers tried different projection systems, but these did not succeed as counter-models. The complex projection of Richard Buckminster Fuller (1895–1983) uses an icosahedron, which is a volume with 20 sides, to try to keep the same proportions in the south and the north. This position is culturally neutral, since there is no top and no bottom. The continents seem to be big islands in the middle of the oceans.

This planisphere certainly inspired the Australians. Contrary to the standards in effect and the influence of centuries of navigation, Australia chose to show itself facing south on its maps. This way, it no longer appears at the edge of the world but floats peacefully over all the countries. Like all things, it is a matter of perspective.

Inverted map of the world: On this map the north is pointed toward the bottom. Along with New Zealand, Australia adopted this type of map a few years ago as a way of rousing national sentiment and of showing that it is possible for any country to appear to be the center of the world. (2002. © ODT, Incorporated.)

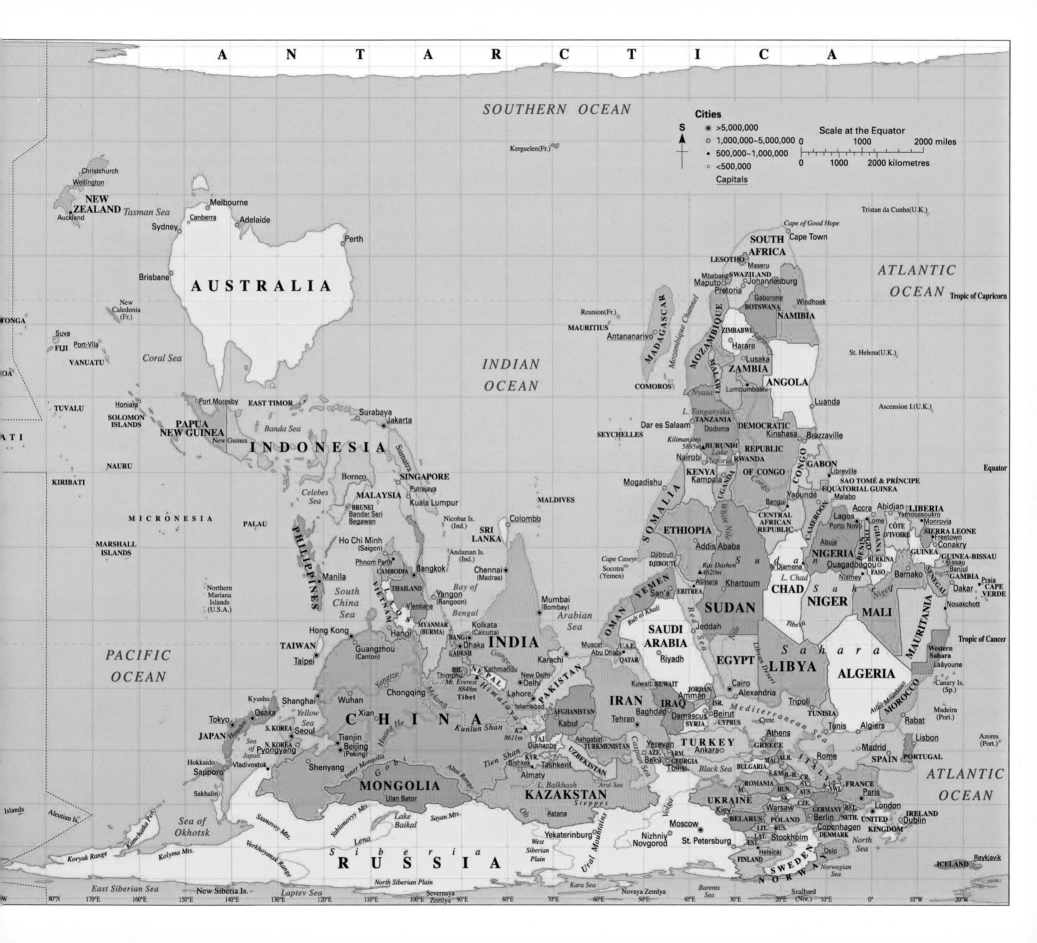

ANTARCTICA

SOUTHERN OCEAN

Cities
● >5,000,000
◉ 1,000,000~5,000,000
• 500,000~1,000,000
○ <500,000
Capitals

Scale at the Equator
0   1000   2000 miles
0   1000   2000 kilometres

Kerguelen(Fr.)

S

Tristan da Cunha(U.K.)

Christchurch
Wellington

NEW
ZEALAND   *Tasman Sea*
Auckland

Melbourne
Canberra
Sydney   Adelaide

Perth

Cape of Good Hope
Cape Town

**SOUTH
AFRICA**

ATLANTIC
OCEAN

LESOTHO   Maseru
Mbabane SWAZILAND
Maputo   Johannesburg
Pretoria

Gaborone
BOTSWANA   Windhoek
NAMIBIA

Tropic of Capricorn

AUSTRALIA

Brisbane

New
Caledonia
(Fr.)

Reunion(Fr.)

MAURITIUS
Antananarivo

ZIMBABWE
Harare

St. Helena(U.K.)

TONGA

Suva
Port-Vila
FIJI
VANUATU

Coral Sea

*INDIAN
OCEAN*

COMOROS

L. Nyasa

MOZAMBIQUE
MALAWI
ZAMBIA   Lusaka

Lumbumbashi

ANGOLA
Luanda

Ascension I.(U.K.)

TUVALU

Honiara
SOLOMON
ISLANDS

Port Moresby
EAST TIMOR

Surabaya
Jakarta

Banda Sea

L. Tanganyika
Dar es Salaam
TANZANIA
Dodoma

DEMOCRATIC

Kinshasa
Brazzaville

Equator

ATI

PAPUA
NEW GUINEA
New Guinea

SEYCHELLES

Kilimanjaro
5895m▲

BURUNDI
Nairobi   Lake

REPUBLIC

CONGO

GABON
Libreville

NAURU

INDONESIA

Sumatra

Victoria

RWANDA

OF CONGO

Congo

SAO TOMÉ & PRÍNCIPE
EQUATORIAL GUINEA

KIRIBATI

Borneo

*Celebes
Sea*

SINGAPORE
Putrajaya
Kuala Lumpur

MALDIVES

KENYA
Kampala
UGANDA

Bangui

Malabo
Yaoundé

MICRONESIA

MALAYSIA

Mogadishu

CENTRAL
AFRICAN
REPUBLIC

Accra   Abidjan
CAMEROON

LIBERIA
Monrovia

PALAU

BRUNEI
Bandar Seri
Begawan

Nicobar Is.
(Ind.)

**SRI
LANKA**

Colombo

SOMALIA

ETHIOPIA
Addis Ababa

NIGERIA
Lagos
Porto Novo

Lomé
GHANA
BENIN
TOGO

CÔTE
D'IVOIRE

Yamoussoukro
SIERRA LEONE
Freetown
Conakry

MARSHALL
ISLANDS

Ho Chi Minh
(Saigon)

Andaman Is.
(Ind.)

Chennai
(Madras)

Cape Caseyr
Socotra
(Yemen)

DJIBOUTI
Djibouti

Asmara
ERITREA

Ras Dashen
▲4620m

Abuja

Ouagadougou
BURKINA
FASO

GUINEA
GUINEA-BISSAU
Bissau
Banjul
GAMBIA

Northern
Mariana
Islands
(U.S.A.)

PHILIPPINES

Phnom Penh
CAMBODIA

Manila

*South
China
Sea*

VIETNAM

Bangkok
THAILAND

Yangon
(Rangoon)

*Bay of
Bengal*

Mumbai
(Bombay)

*Arabian
Sea*

YEMEN
San'a

Rub' al Khali

Khartoum

Jeddah

SUDAN

CHAD
N'Djamena
L. Chad

Niamey

Sahel

Bamako
Niger

Dakar

SENEGAL

Praia
CAPE
VERDE

Nouakchott

Hong Kong

Guangzhou
(Canton)

Vientiane
LAOS

MYANMAR
(BURMA)

BANG.
Dhaka

Kolkata
(Calcutta)

INDIA

Karachi

OMAN
Muscat
U.A.E.
Abu Dhabi

**SAUDI
ARABIA**
Riyadh

Red Sea

Nile

EGYPT

LIBYA

Sahara

NIGER

MALI

MAURITANIA

Western
Sahara

Tropic of Cancer

TAIWAN

Taipei

Hanoi

Ganges

BH.
Thimphu
Mt. Everest
8848m
Tibet

NEPAL
Kathmandu

BLADESH

New Delhi
Delhi

Kunlun Shan

Kabul

Chongqing

Mekong

Himalaya

Yangtze

Wuhan

Xian

CHINA

Islamabad
Lahore
PAKISTAN

QATAR

KUWAIT
Kuwait

AFGHANISTAN

Indus

K2
8611m

Ashgabat

JORDAN
Amman

Baghdad
IRAQ

Mediterranean

Cairo

Alexandria

TUNISIA
Tunis

Tripoli

Atlas Mountains

ALGERIA

MOROCCO

Canary Is.
(Sp.)

Rabat

Madeira
(Port.)

*PACIFIC
OCEAN*

Kyushu

Shanghai

*Yellow
Sea*

Tokyo   Osaka
Honshu
JAPAN
S. KOREA
Seoul

*Sea of
Japan*

Tianjin
Beijing
(Peking)

Shenyang

Kyrgyzstan

IRAN
Tehran

TAJ.
Dushanbe
KYR.
Bishkek

Damascus
SYRIA
Beirut
ISR.
CYPRUS

Tien Shan

Tashkent

Almaty

UZBEKISTAN

Baku
AZE.
ARM.
Yerevan
GEORGIA
Tbilisi

TURKEY
Ankara

Crete

Athens

GREECE

Rome

ITALY

Algiers

Lisbon

SPAIN   PORTUGAL

Madrid

Azores
(Port.)

ATLANTIC
OCEAN

Hokkaido
Sapporo

N. KOREA
Pyongyang

Huang He

Gobi

Altai Range

Caspian Sea

MAC. ALB.
BULGARIA

S&M B.H.
CR.

France
Paris

Vladivostok

Inner Mongolia

MONGOLIA
Ulan Bator

Steppes

Aral Sea

KAZAKSTAN

L. Balkhash

M.
ROMANIA
HUN.
SV.
SLK.
AUS.
SWI.

Islands

Alcutian Is.

*Sea of
Okhotsk*

Kamchatka Pen.

Stanovoy Mts.

*Lake
Baikal*

Sayan Mts.

Ob

Astana

Volga

UKRAINE
Kiev

Warsaw

CZE.

BEL.

GERMANY
Berlin
NETH.

London

UNITED
KINGDOM

IRELAND
Dublin

Koryak Range

Kolyma Mts.

Verkhoyansk Range

Lena

Siberia

Yablonovyy Mts.

West
Siberian
Plain

Yekaterinburg

Ural Mountains

Nizhniy
Novgorod

Moscow

St. Petersburg

BELARUS
LIT.
RUS.
LAT.
EST.

Poland

Copenhagen
DENMARK

North
Sea

East Siberian Sea

New Siberia Is.

Laptev Sea

Severnaya
Zemlya

North Siberian Plain

RUSSIA

Kara Sea

Novaya Zemlya

*Barents
Sea*

Svalbard
(Nor.)

Helsinki
FINLAND

Stockholm

SWEDEN
Oslo

Norwegian
Sea

ICELAND
Reykjavik

80°N 170°E 160°E 150°E 140°E 130°E 120°E 110°E 100°E 90°E 80°E 70°E 60°E 50°E 40°E 30°E 20°E 10°E 0° 10°W 20°W

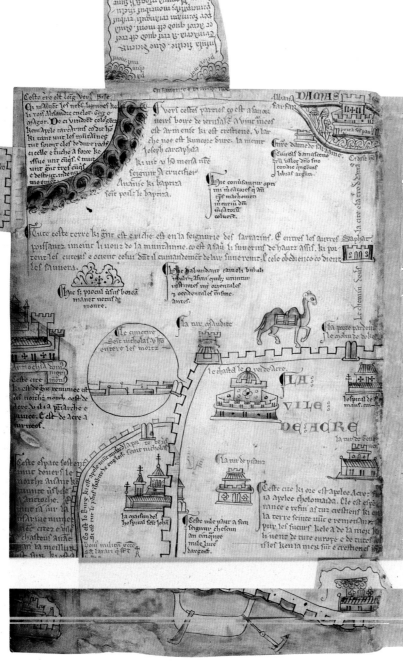

Route from London to Jerusalem.
(13th century. The British Library, London.)

Traveling the World

To say that one needed the domestication of a placid camelid in order to cross the deserts and roads worthy of this name in order to travel long distances is an understatement (roads, or at least simple tracks, if one believes the historians, even when they evoke the symbolism of the Silk Road). However, if the reputation of this trade gives the impression of intense and uninterrupted traffic, the convoys that linked the Far East to the Middle East, from Chang'an in China to Antioch in Syria, arranged several stops in oases. These were the points where all the routes and all the travelers converged: pilgrims, soldiers and spies.

It was the Romans who started the trade in silk, which was manufactured exclusively by the Chinese, when they discovered it at the beginning of the 1st millennium. But other merchandise changed hands on these same roads: precious stones and metals, wool, linen, amber, ivory, lacquer, spices, glass, coral and more. However, the Silk Road was abandoned in the 15th century.

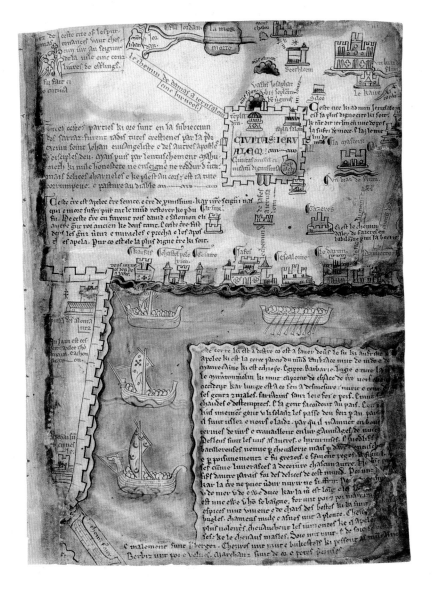

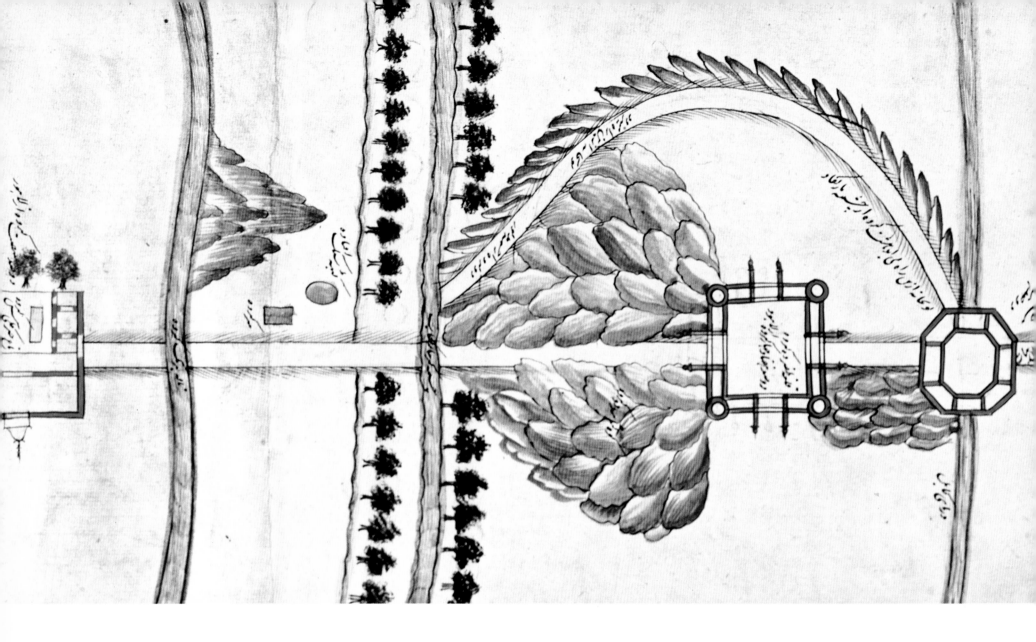

Each empire developed its own means of transportation and trade. Moreover, the empires with the most solid networks were the most powerful. Yet, before there were roads, trade took place on rivers, lakes and seas. In the 7th century BCE, the Egyptians developed canals and a system of locks to ensure the transportation of people and goods, in particular between the Nile and the Red Sea. The invention of the wheel (3500 BCE) at Sumer in Lower Mesopotamia helped to add streets, paths and roads to the earth's

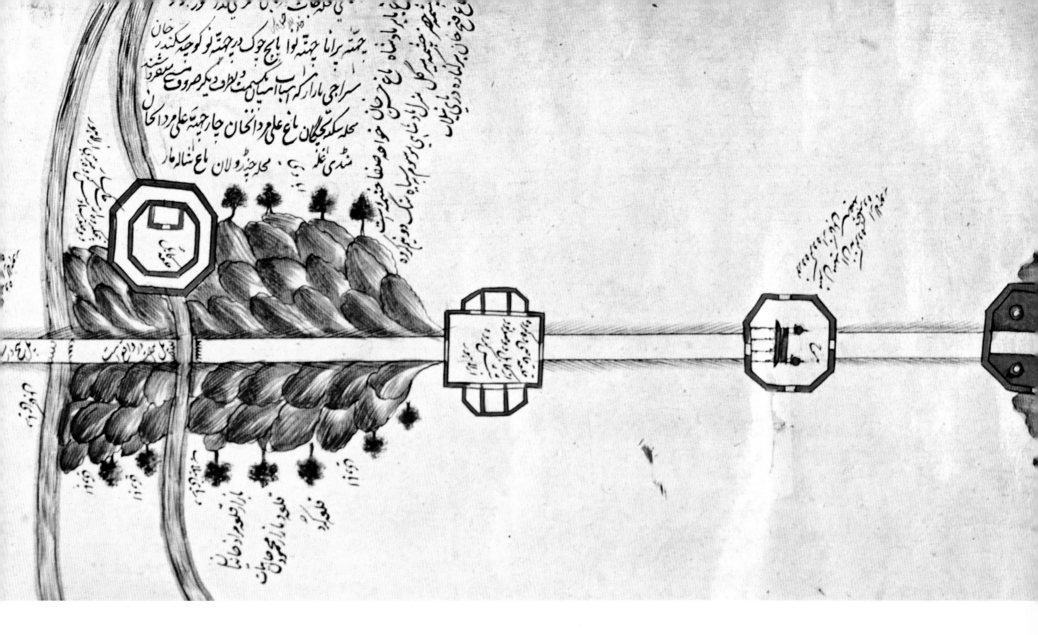

system of navigation. Carts pulled by people, donkeys or oxen took care of the portages. The Romans were known for having very practical surveyors, so much so that their maps were called "tables." Vegetius, the author of a military treaty, boasted in the 4th century of having several maps that showed distances in numbers of feet, specified trails and indicated shortcuts, mountains, streams and the possibilities of where to stop and lodge — a veritable tourist map before its time.

This Persian manuscript by Nasu Peroar shows a map of the route from New Delhi, India, to Kandahar, Afghanistan. (The British Library, London.)

*B*ritannia, published in England during the 17th century, is considered the first road "atlas." Created by John Ogilby, it recorded 7,500 miles (12,070 km) of routes with a precision unknown until its time: bridge construction materials, barriers, the direction of a slope, hedges and fences were all recorded in detail. This book was so successful that it was republished in a pocket-book format for a larger public. Moreover, at this time there was also a flurry of new routes under construction.

In Russia, exchanges progressed as well. When Ambassador Starkoff brought tea back to the court of the czar, a new trade began between his country and China, and whole caravans were soon importing it, as the drink was highly valued. The great tea route was thus born. From Irkutsk, Siberia, the tea crossed the Bouriat territory and Lake Baikal for more than a year and over approximately 6,200 miles (10,000 km).

Russia: "Saint Petersburg–Moscow train route, built in 1842, and waterways," a map showing the direction of the railroad. (1844. Postal Museum, Berlin.)

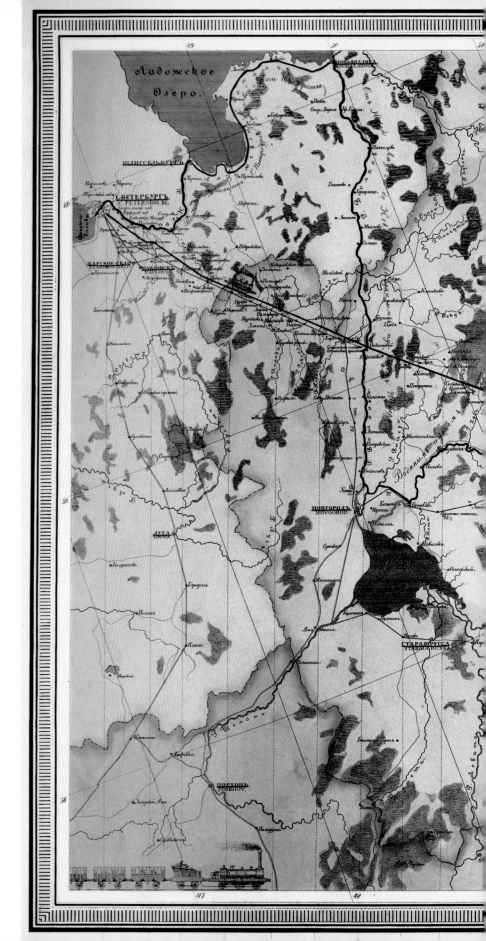

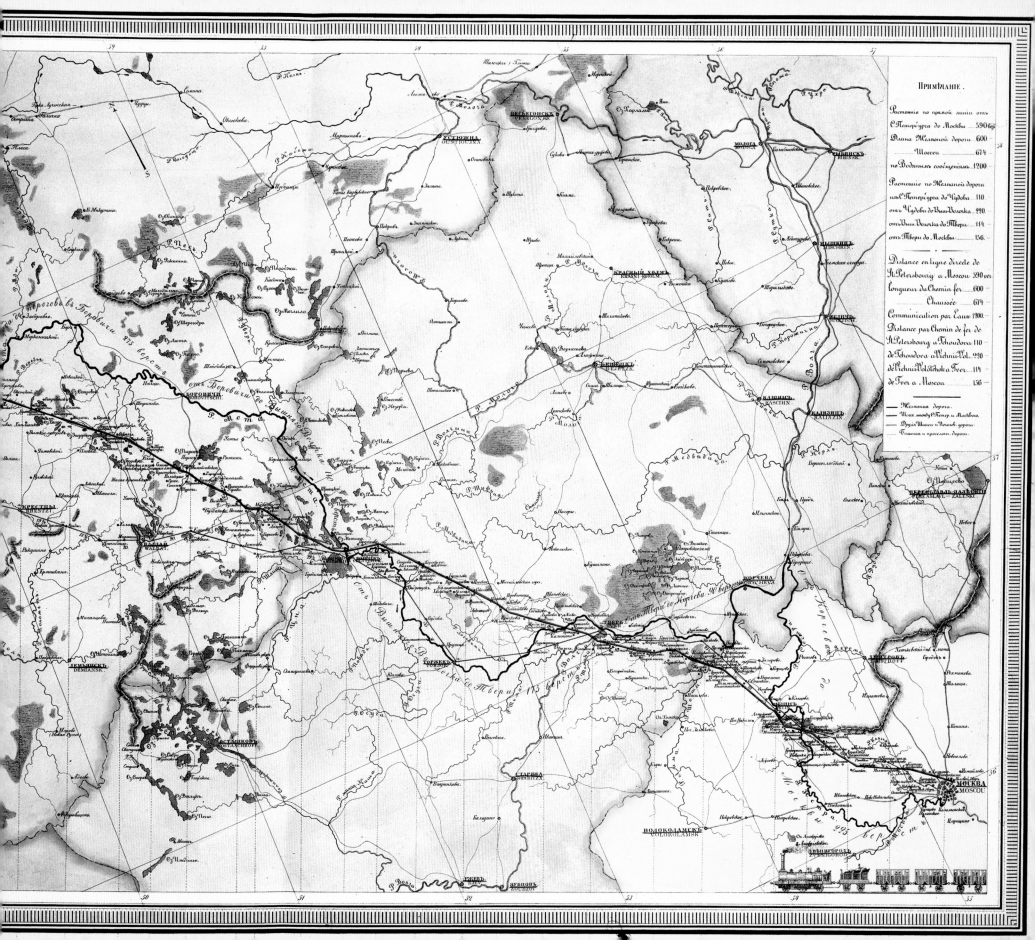

ПРИМѢЧАНІЕ.

Разстояніе по прямой линіи отъ
С.Петербурга до Москвы   590 вер.
Длина Желѣзной дороги   600 —
Шоссе   674 —
по Водянымъ сообщеніямъ 1200 —

Разстояніе по Желѣзной дорогѣ
изъ С.Петербурга до Чудова 110 —
отъ Чудова до Вышн.Волочка 220 —
отъ Вышн.Волочка до Твери 114 —
отъ Твери до Москвы   156 —

Distance en ligne directe de
St.Petersbourg a Moscou   590 ver.
longueur du Chemin fer   600 —
Chaussée   674 —
Communication par Eaux 1200 —

Distance par Chemin de fer de
St.Petersbourg a Tchoudova 110 —
de Tchoudova a Vichni.Vol. 220 —
de Vichni.Volotchka a Tver 114 —
de Tver a Moscou   156 —

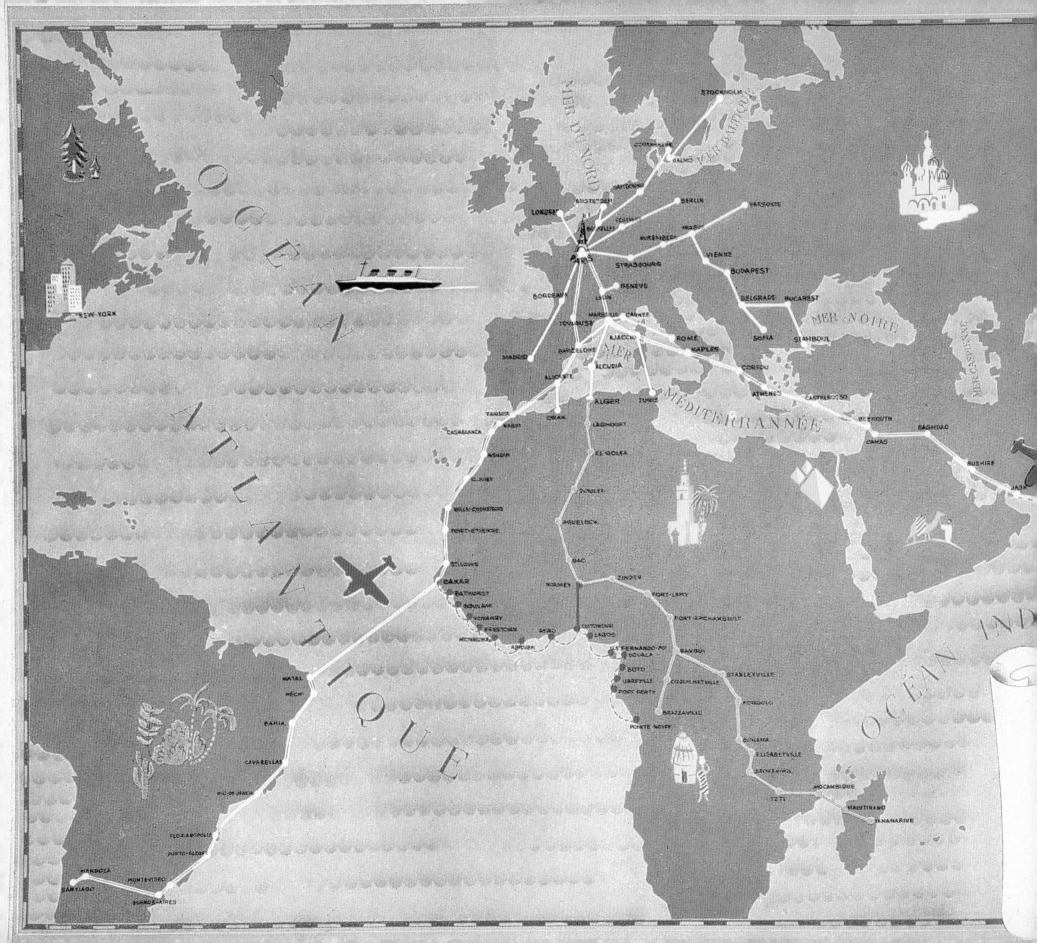

ligne AIR FRANCE

ligne RÉGIE AIR AFRIQUE

ligne AÉRO-MARITIME
(PROJET)

LEFT: *The imperial lines of French aviation. (1936.)*

FOLLOWING DOUBLE PAGE: *Hand-drawn map of Mont Blanc based on photographs taken on the ground. (1953. With the kind permission of the National Geographic Institute.)*

Both the men who transported the merchandise and the merchants felt the need to categorize these new routes to facilitate travel. In the 19th century, railroads followed closely behind land routes and constituted numerous transportation plans. Transportation companies produced these railroad plans, and their goal was to encourage new travelers to use their lines. Like those posted in railway stations, these maps were often produced in a small format for customers. In cities, the arrival of new means of transportation required a certain standardization so that the streetcar, horse-drawn bus and trolleybus systems could be shown on the same map. In the United States, some regions saw in these maps a way to promote their territory and attract settlers and visitors. Maps started to show everything that a country had to offer. In magazines and newspapers, and on stamps and even in Bibles, the world was displayed in the form of streets, routes and roads. A century later, the sky was also mapped, and airplanes were ready to fly toward new horizons.

The Conquest of Space

And beyond?

"From the scrubby valley, white rocks emerge;
Scattered in the cold sky, some red foliage …
On the narrow path from the mountain, it did not rain;
But the azure of the space floods my clothes."

Wang Wei, The Mountain

hen looking at the sky, one's gaze moves above the horizon, and what one looks for in that immense space is as much the home of the gods as that of one's ancestors and the righteous.

Could it be that down below, where the soil is worked by hand and where the dead sleep, is so familiar that somewhere else, somewhere bigger and higher, is needed for the final voyage? In the past, when a Romany man died, they cut the hair from his horse's mane and slipped it into the coffin so that he could travel the road to heaven — for how would he know where he was going without his companion?

According to the Vedas, the sacred texts of Hindus, the Organizer gave shape to "the Sun and the Moon, in order of priority, then the Heavens and the Earth, the Air and, finally, the Light." Mystics have sung for a long time about god unfolding the sky like a nomadic tent, the fabric of the world, a protective roof or a shroud that envelops the night. Even once people knew how to push back the limits of the world and to defy space and time, could they forget that first innate gesture, the simple act of raising one's eyes to the sky, that inaccessible vault where each month the moon dies and is reborn, and each day the sun is lit and extinguished?

In Greek Antiquity, some imagined that the sky was blue because the universe was a huge bubble filled with air and water on which the earth floated — it could not be floating on nothing. Heraklides theorized the Earth turns on its own axis every 24 hours, and Aristarchus explained that it revolves around the sun, the center of the universe, and not the reverse. But it was still the deities, the first being Zeus, who governed the world order, so who would listen to them? Nicholas Copernicus, 18 centuries later. And today, all that remains to be known is how far the sky extends its billions of galaxies.

Climbing to the Sky

Humans have long searched for the holy mountain, the central pillar, the hearth, the axis or the ladder that would allow them to communicate with the celestial world. There were those who believed that what exists in the world below should have its perfect replica in the world above. According to Mircea Eliade, for the Mesopotamians, "the Tigris is modeled on the star Anunit and the Euphrates on the star of the Owl." The stars were signs and markers for them. They regulated the time of human, religious and agricultural activities, announced the floods, the dog days of summer and the frost, and marked the moment of the migrations and the time to sow the fields. It was with the phases of the moon and the rising and setting of the sun that the seasons passed and time was measured.

Air in his chest, water in his body — man, as Hildegard of Bingen saw him, is in harmony with the cosmos because he is its double: "Look inside you, you are the sky and the earth." Humans saw themselves in the image of the universe, as a small world all to themselves, both sky and earth. The best proof of this was that a human head is round like the sky, the seven orifices are like the seven planets and our two eyes are like the moon and the sun. How could one not believe that what happens on the earth is surely caused by something in the sky, there where the gods who govern the stars reside? And the planets, how could they not influence birth and death?

The Shepherd's Star, which guided the herds of stars in the Milky Way as well as the navigators' boats on the swells of the high seas, lay next to the evil star and the shooting star, the sign of happiness. The sky was a somewhere else, where fate played a role. It was a home to return to through a slow spiritual climb to finally contemplate God, the seven celestial levels, the seven degrees of the soul and the seven days of creation crowned by seventh heaven. Everything was believed to be connected in a matching game.

China: Map of the stars that are visible from the northern hemisphere. (Created between 618 and 906. The British Library, London.)

自氐二度樹辰盡尾七度於辰在丑角亢星記者言統已萬物之終故

越之分也

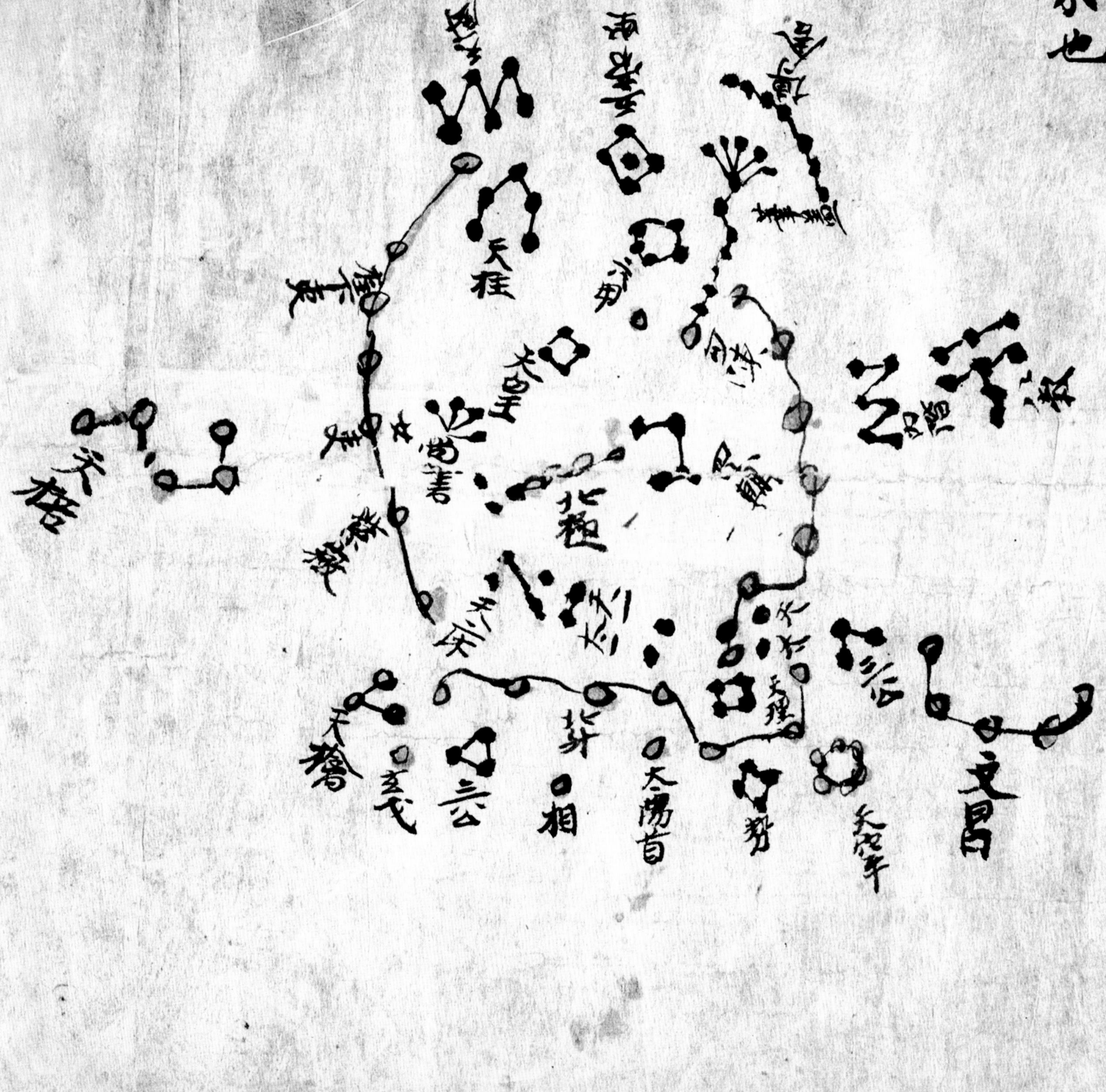

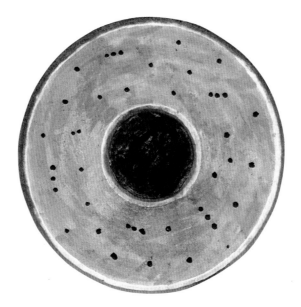

In the sky of Antiquity, the one the astrologers observed for the kings and the powerful, few stars could be observed due to a lack of instruments, but what was certain was that humans were at the center of the universe and that everything revolved around them.

It is said that Jason was offered the first celestial globe so he could successfully lead his high-seas expedition with the Argonauts and bring back the Golden Fleece. The complicity of a centaur was required to allow humans to learn the secrets of the heavens, but did the centaur not also transform his daughter, Hippe, into a constellation? It is mythical stories that gave the constellations their outlines drawn using starry points, and each culture drew its own, seeing in the sky horses, rats, pigs, hares, agricultural implements, ships for navigators or arms for hunters. For the Mongols, who were a horse-riding people, the North Star is the nail in the sky to which all horses are hitched.

The twins and the constellations from the Book of the Sky, *an Ottoman manuscript. (16th century. Istanbul University Library.)*

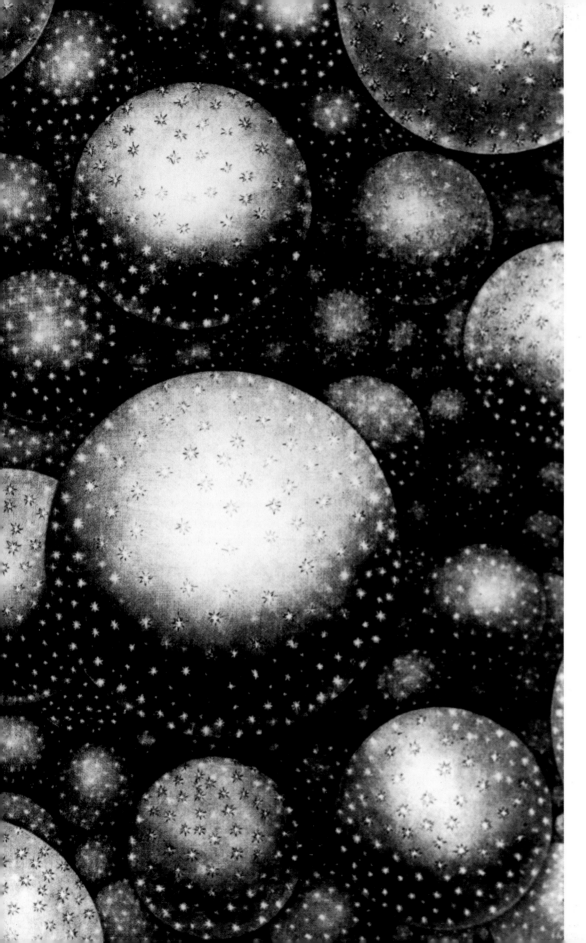

Draco, the dragon constellation, which appears in the spring, has a long history: it is the story of Marduk, the giant dragon, god of the Babylonians and conqueror of the monsters of Chaos led by Tiamat. After knocking Tiamat down, Marduk cut him in half. With one half of his enemy's body he created the earth, and with the other the sun and the moon. Next, he inlaid the brilliant North Star and drew, with the stars that were all around, the shape of Tiamat. Thus was born the constellation Draco in the sky.

The names of the stars — like Venus, Vega, Altair, Sirius, Phoenix, Grus and Tucana — were the bearers of earlier dreams. Thousands of years later, they became simple order numbers in a catalog or a series of numbers corresponding to their coordinates. It would take painters and poets to reconquer the celestial space and to interpret these luminous points drawn on the canvas of the sky, like so many question marks on the greatness and finiteness of human beings.

LEFT: *Plate 31 from An Original Theory or New Hypothesis of the Universe by Thomas Wright. (1750. Private collection.)*

RIGHT: *Obscure celestial cartography, an extract from the Atlas céleste (Celestial atlas) by Charles Dien. (1877. National Library of France, Paris.)*

Gauthier-Villars, Libraire Éditeur, Paris.

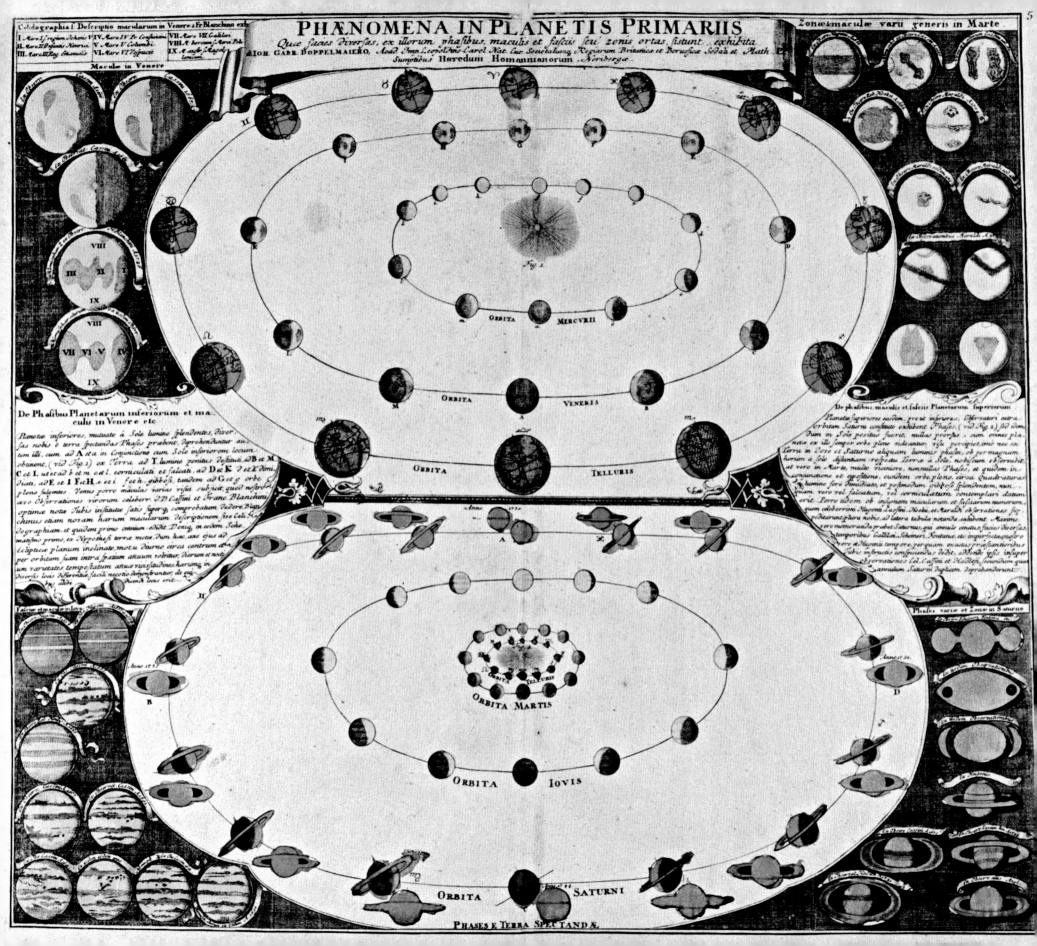

PHÆNOMENA IN PLANETIS PRIMARIIS

Quæ facies diversas, ex illorum phasibus, maculis et falcis seu zonis ortas, sistunt, exhibita à IOH. GABR. DOPPELMAIERO, Acad. Imp. Leopoldino-Carol. Nat. Cur. Societalium, Regiarum Britanicae et Borussicae Sodali et Math.

Sumptibus Haeredum Homannianorum Norimbergae

Selenographia I. Descriptio macularum in Venere a Fr. Blanchino ext.

Zonae et maculae varii generis in Marte.

Maculae in Venere.

ORBITA MERCVRII

ORBITA VENERIS

ORBITA TELLURIS

De Phasibus Planetarum inferiorum et maculis in Venere etc.

De phasibus, maculis et falcis Planetarum superiorum.

ORBITA MARTIS

ORBITA IOVIS

ORBITA SATURNI

PHASES E TERRA SPECTANDÆ

Head in the Clouds

The ancient Greeks believed the cosmos was a sphere because they could see circles in the sky: the elliptical circle described by the Earth on the celestial sphere during its revolution around the sun, and a circle where the constellations of the zodiac were located. And without the sky there could be no geography because, as Ptolemy explained, "geography divides the Earth according to the circles in the sky." Ptolemy's three great works, *Almagest* (on astronomy), *Tetrabible* (on astrology) and *Geography*, required broad knowledge to understand the universe. They also bore witness to a willingness to represent the universe as a whole, which was understood through a clever cogwheel of correlations, an endless journey over the earth and in the sky by the eyes and by reason.

Walking with a lady friend on a beautiful, starry night, Fontenelle (1657–1757) took a chance on a little philosophizing.

To the marchioness who asked him "Tell me about your stars," he answered, "All philosophy … is based on two things only: curiosity and poor eyesight; if you had better eyesight you could see perfectly well whether or not these stars are solar systems, and if you were less curious you wouldn't care about knowing, which amounts to the same thing. The trouble is, we want to know more than what we can see."

Out of courtesy, after having denounced those who admire nature because they believe in a kind of magic which they do not understand, Fontenelle continued: "Madame, you are so willing to understand everything I wish to say to you that I believe I only need to pull back the curtain and show you the world." Once again, in order to take part in the spectacle of the world, not only is a scientific eye required, but so are the necessary tools to see what cannot be seen.

Representation of the motion of the planets around the sun from the Atlas Coelestis by Johann Gabriel Doppelmayr, published in Nuremberg. (1742. Private Collection.)

Since Antiquity, people have known how to calculate the latitude of a point based on the position of the sun or a star above the horizon using an instrument such as a simple astrolabe or cross-staff. Yet, for almost 2,000 years, as surprising as this may seem, observation instruments have changed little, and Nicholas Copernicus (1473–1543) used the same instruments as Ptolemy (90–168) — namely the quadrant, the triquetrum and the armillary sphere. Through its graduated metal rings representing the principal circles of the elliptical sky — the equator, the tropics and the meridians — the armillary sphere helped to make the sky more intelligible. In the center of it lay the earth before it was established that, in reality, it revolves around the sun.

For those who contemplate the sky, how can one know where one is without any maps of this immense space? Yet, since by looking at the sky one can imagine it as a vault that adjusts to the earth, the sky is represented on a sphere, as a globe. The stars and planets were observed and were positioned along fundamental circles. And, from the moment when the roundness of the earth is demonstrated, what could be better for a scholar at the forefront of his time than to possess two globes: sky and Earth?

The motion of the sun as studied by an astronomer using an armillary sphere and a quadrant. (16th century. Ottoman manuscript. Istanbul University Library, Turkey.)

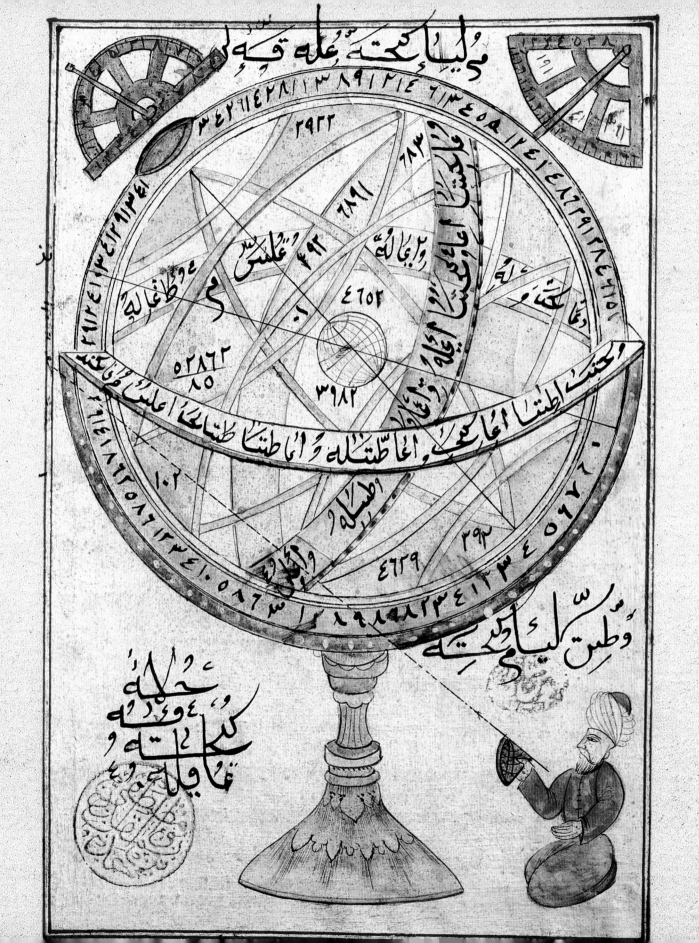

In the past, the appearance of an unknown star was always disconcerting, but it was also an occasion to update star maps. What could such a phenomenon mean: a threat, the announcement of a great birth, a pending death? The Chinese emperor's astronomers had to inform him day or night of the motion of the stars and the divine signs. The Chinese had imagined a sky that resembled their society, one in which the celestial emperor watched over his subjects from his upper palace on the North Star. The earthly emperor had to do the same and ensure harmony within his empire. In 1054, the approach of a bright star over China was, therefore, an extraordinary event for Chinese astronomers. They named it "Welcome" and reported it on all their star maps, in its place in the constellation of Taurus. Soon, their star lost its shine and disappeared. The astronomers' amazement turned into consternation: what did the soothsayers have to reveal and how is such a phenomenon possible? What if all the stars disappeared? Faced with such a hypothesis, it is said that the Chinese astronomers increased their observations and their maps became more accurate.

On November 11, 1577, while observing the appearance in the sky just above the moon of a new star that remained stationary for months, Tycho Brahe (1546–1601) understood that Aristotle had been wrong: the supra-lunar world was not constant. It was high time, he thought, to free himself from this tradition and from Ptolemy at the same time.

While Tycho Brahe believed that Copernicus was right about the planets revolving around the sun, he still believed that the sun, for its part, revolved around the earth. Johannes Kepler (1571–1630), who knew Tycho Brahe's measurements well, refuted this claim: he showed that the sun, not the earth, is the center of the world. From that moment on, it was no longer possible for astronomers to trust the ancient scholars, and they also felt an obligation to criticize and review tradition if it was not in keeping with observed reality.

While astronomers were seeking a new world system in the stars, in 1610 everything changed. Galileo (1564–1642) may have heard about a spyglass that was being made in Holland, or he may have just received one, it is not known exactly. Either way, once in his

Motion of the Moon from Liber Floridus *by Lambert de Saint-Omer. 15th century. Condé Museum, Chantilly, France.)*

possession, he quickly pointed his spyglass toward the sky. This glass owed nothing to the science of optics but was the product of ingenious tinkering by a craftsman amused by natural magic: it was a matter of bringing distant objects closer using concave and convex glass.

Galileo invented a new spyglass that magnified eight to nine times. He declared that he had made it because he understood how useful it would be for land-based business as well as for use on the sea. It was not yet a matter of astronomy for him, but making inventions that would allow him and his family to survive. He offered his first spyglass to the Venitians, who certainly understood its military usefulness. Soon the grand duke of Florence and his brother, the duke de' Medici, each wanted their own.

Galileo then produced a spyglass capable of magnifying 20 times, and he began to observe the heavenly bodies in a systematic way: the mountains on the moon, the four satellites of Jupiter, the phases of Venus, a moving sun. In a book entitled *The Starry Messenger*, he sent his first results to his Serene Highness Cosimo II, the fourth grand duke of Tuscany and duke de' Medici. In this book, Galileo notes that he is constantly discovering new stars and that he cannot name or draw them because they are so numerous. He was at the point where he would produce a spyglass capable of magnifying 30 times, making it possible to observe the moon more closely. In his book, Galileo also states that the earth wanders and that a work on the truth of this theory will soon be published to support his claims.

Before Galileo's famous spyglass, the astronomer al-Battani (858–929), who lived in Raqqa in the north of what is now Syria, systematically watched the sky using so-called observation tubes that were said to help focus the eye on a corner of the sky by eliminating stray light. This instrument arrived in the West as early as the 10th century. Al-Battani had a huge impact on medieval astronomy in Europe because his monumental work, the *Zidj*, is the only scientific treaty to have been translated into Latin as early as the 12th century. He was considered the greatest Arab astronomer.

From the Earth to the Moon

Since the time of Galileo, the moon has assumed a whole other landscape because, with its continents, mountains, seas and craters, it resembles the Earth. The moon, the first reference to calculate the passage of time by using its four different shapes, thereby lost its constant and eternal status. And, while in China one saw it as the home of a rabbit or a toad, elsewhere people asked themselves how, if it was inhabited, one could reach it without offending God and his angels. Or was it a perfect mirror image of the earth or perhaps the place to which souls migrated after death?

The moon has always made people dream. Is this why its seas were given evocative names like Serenity, Vapors, Fertility, Moisture and Clouds? As for the Ocean of Storms, how could it not spark the imaginations of novelists and make them dream of lunar voyages? People may ask themselves who provided these names and who validated them so that the face of the moon could be drawn. The first lunar map was published by the Dutch astronomer and geographer Michael Florent Langrenus (1598–1675). He was the first, in his book *Plenilunium*, to name 332 different details on this star. In assigning names, he did not forget King Philip IV of Spain, who had allowed him to publish his observations. An ocean and a crater would bear the name of his benefactor up to the sky. And why not also have his own moment of glory by baptizing a lunar feature in his name? The Langrenus Crater is the epitome of the best way for an astronomer to be remembered forever.

The short history of astronomy says that on February 12, 1679, Giovanni Cassini (1625–1712), the first astronomer of the Cassini dynasty to manage the Royal Observatory in Paris, presented his map of the moon, which was engraved on copper by Jean Patigny, to the Academy of Sciences. A moment of honor, an honest effort and, no doubt, the fruit of many hours of observation, but not one without its controversies: hidden in the relief of the moon, he slid the face of his wife. Some saw in it a declaration of his love, others the more symbolic link of this star with femininity and fertility. Could the moon have secrets that scientific reason enjoys hiding?

Selenographia sive lunae descriptio
(Selenography, or a description of the
moon) by Johannes Hevelius
(17th century. National Library of France.)

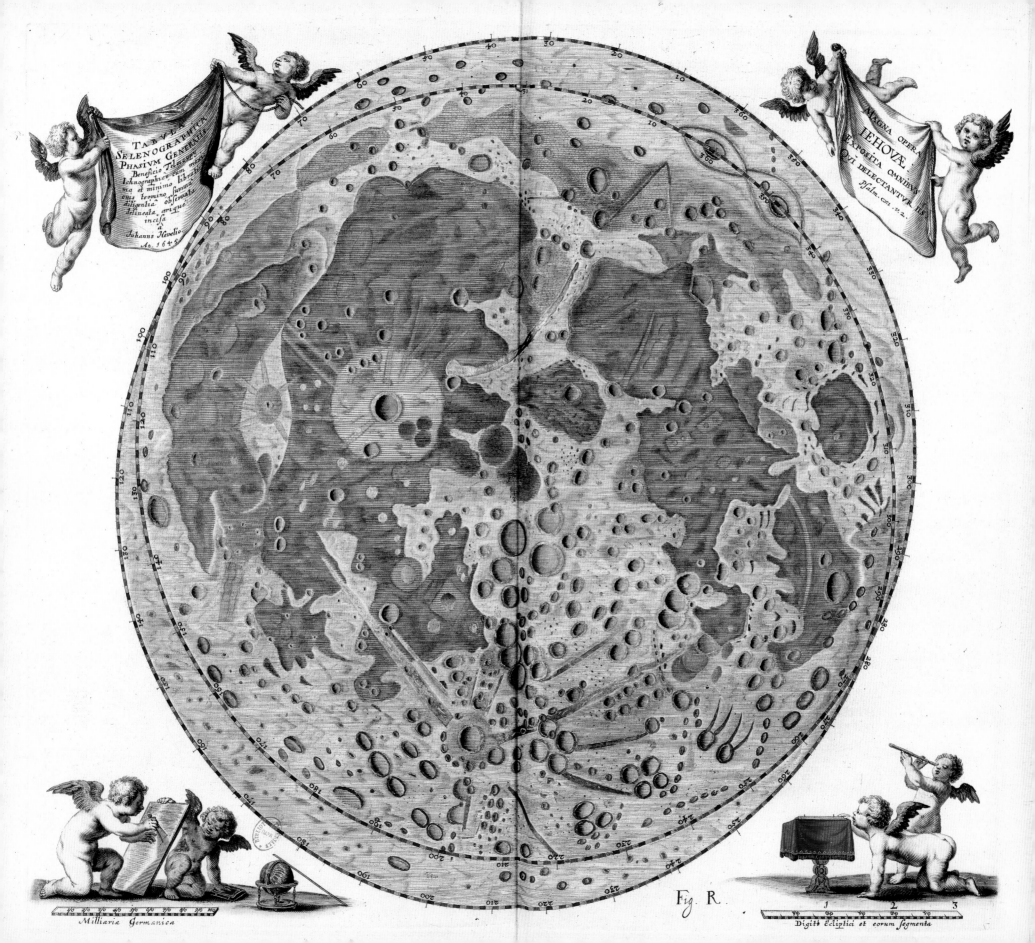

TABULA
SELENOGRAPHICA
PHASIUM GENERALIS
Beneficio Telescopii
Ichnographice, cum maxi-
ma et minimo Libratio-
nis termino summa
diligentia observata
delineata, ærique
incisa
a
Johanne Hevelio.
Ao. 1645.

MAGNA OPERA
IEHOVÆ,
EXPOSITA OMNIBVS,
QVI DELECTANTVR IIS.
Psalm. cxi. 2.2.

Fig. R.

Milliaria Germanica

Digiti Ecliptici et eorum segmenta

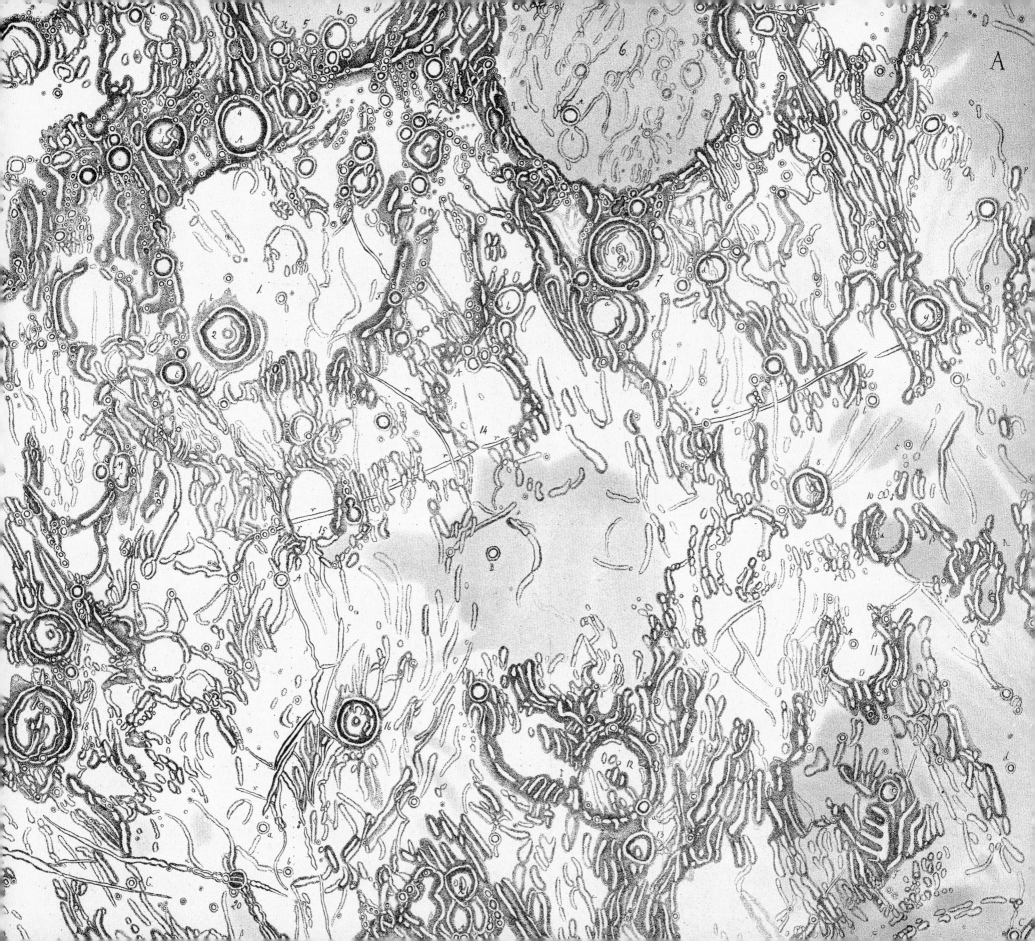

The construction of observatories and better astronomical spyglasses soon allowed for more detailed lunar maps, but each cartographer chose, completely subjectively, the name for such and such a crater that he had just recorded. So much so that the same feature can have several names. Famous scholars, such as Copernicus and Ptolemy, or generous monarchs had the right to have their name on the moon. Three astronomers, Riccioli (1598–1671), Grimaldi (1618–1663) and Hevelius (1611–1687), contributed to the 17th century by marking lunar space in Latin, thereby making it more familiar, with its Carpathian and Apennine mountains. And the discoveries and the names kept coming. We knew nothing about the dark side of the moon before 1959, when the Soviet probe Luna 3 revealed its images. And so, to the Sea of Serenity on the visible side was added the Mare Moscoviense, the Sea of Moscow.

We had to explore all of our planet's roads, grid all the fields and mark all the oceans before seeking out other unknowns in space. Setting foot on the moon was an extraordinary adventure and a way to, yet again, push back the limits of our knowledge. But, as Pascal would have said, what is man in the infinite? Not much, but on the moon, men and women can always and forever be dreamers. With these human sentiments shared, perhaps unknowingly, with Cassini, the American astronauts did not hesitate to give some lunar formations the names of their wives. Far away and elsewhere, there is a need to feel reassured by what is near and dear.

Plate 1 from Charte der Gebirge des Mondes
(Chart of the mountains of the moon) by Julius Schmidt.
(1878. National Library of France, Paris.)

Views from Above

When the photographer Felix Tournachon (1820–1910), better known as Nadar, summarized the work of cartographers, he spoke of the huge amount of work that went into creating the land register with an army of engineers, surveyors, chainmen, artists and calculators who took a half-century to do the job and did it badly. He went on to claim that within 30 days he could complete the work by himself and do it perfectly. He called a good aerostat that was connected to the ground and a good camera his only weapons. Nadar, who made lighter cameras so he could take them on trips, had just given himself a new challenge. It had already been several years since, captivated by his balloon rides, he had been thinking of a way to profit from their use. After his first aerial photograph of Paris, over the Petit-Bicêtre, he was determined to pursue the venture. In 1863, he had a balloon, Le Géant (The Giant), built by his new company, the Société d'encouragement de la navigation aérienne au moyen du plus lourd que l'air (the Society for the Encouragement of Aerial Locomotion by the Means of Heavier than Air Machines). In 1870, the photographer finally saw a way to demonstrate the usefulness of his project by putting it at the disposal of the government during the German siege of Paris. His Compagnie d'aérostiers (Aerostat Pilots Company) helped to monitor the enemy and to deliver the mail, but mostly it established cartographical landmarks.

Aerial photograph of Gironde, France.
(With the kind permission of the
National Geographic Institute.)

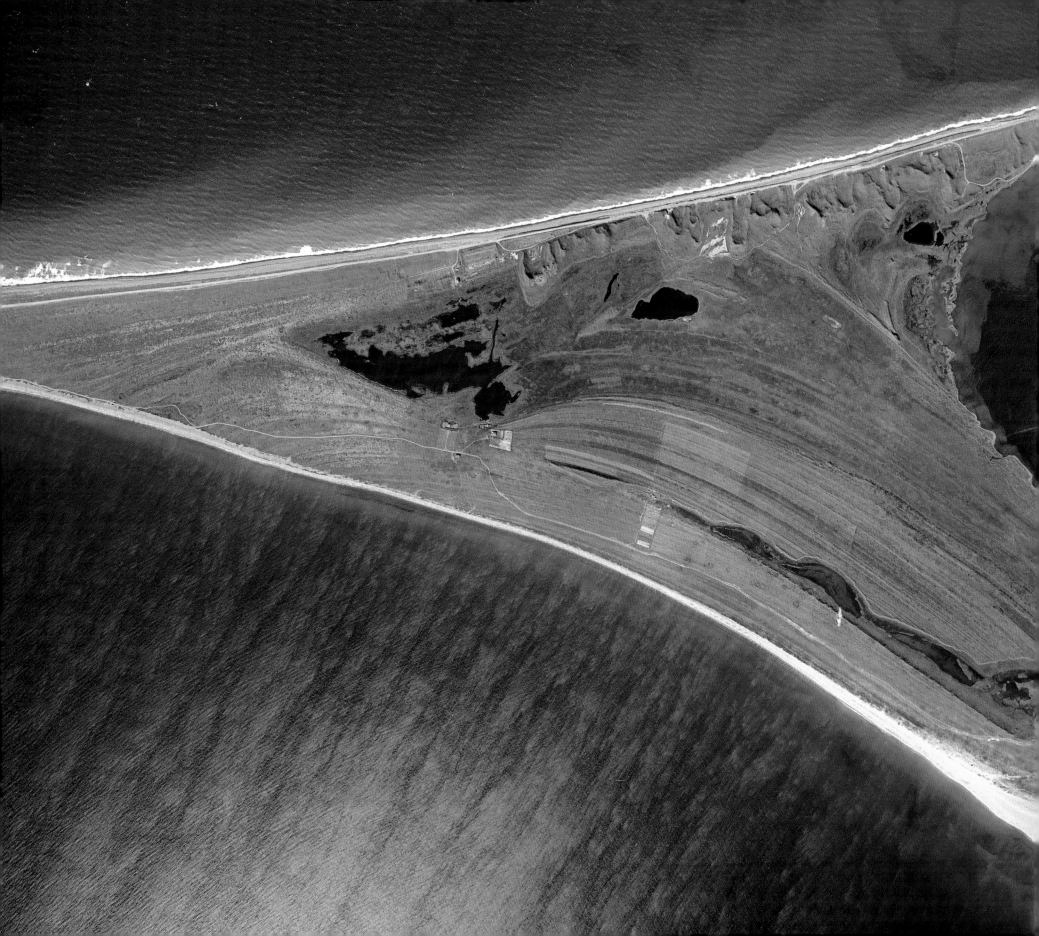

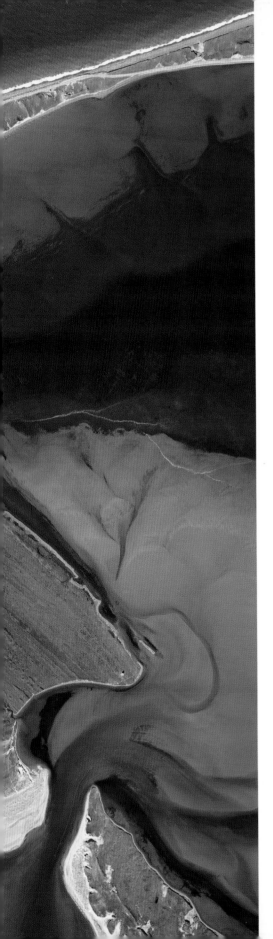

A little later, in 1909, it truly became possible to talk about aerial photographs thanks to the aviator Wilbur Wright. The cameras had also improved. The advent of a mechanism that allowed for continuous photographs improved speed and the variety of shots, producing highly accurate results. The military, which supported aerial cartography, proposed innovations of its own as early as 1914. The maps could help soldiers plan their shots and prepare their attacks.

It took the end of the Second World War to see what civilian use could be made of these innovations and to go beyond surveillance and reconnaissance — the space age was launched. The Soviets and Americans launched their satellites, Sputnik (1957), Explorer 6 (1959) and Discoverer 13 (1960), to attack the sky and space. Against the backdrop of these "star wars," earthlings could finally see images of their planet taken from a distance. Politicians claimed scientists were studying the layers of cloud, the inaccessible regions like the polar circles and the peculiar shape of the globe (flat on the top and the bottom), while, at the same time, the military was planning the minute details of how to best direct nuclear missiles. Protected behind scientific observations, the enemy became almost omniscient, proud of their machines that revolved endlessly, like impregnable citadels at the outer limits of the sky.

OPPOSITE: *Aerial photograph of Saint-Pierre and Miquelon, France. (With the kind permission of the National Geographic Institute.)*

FOLLOWING DOUBLE PAGE: *Satellite image of Denmark, Greenland and the King Oscar Fjord.*

181

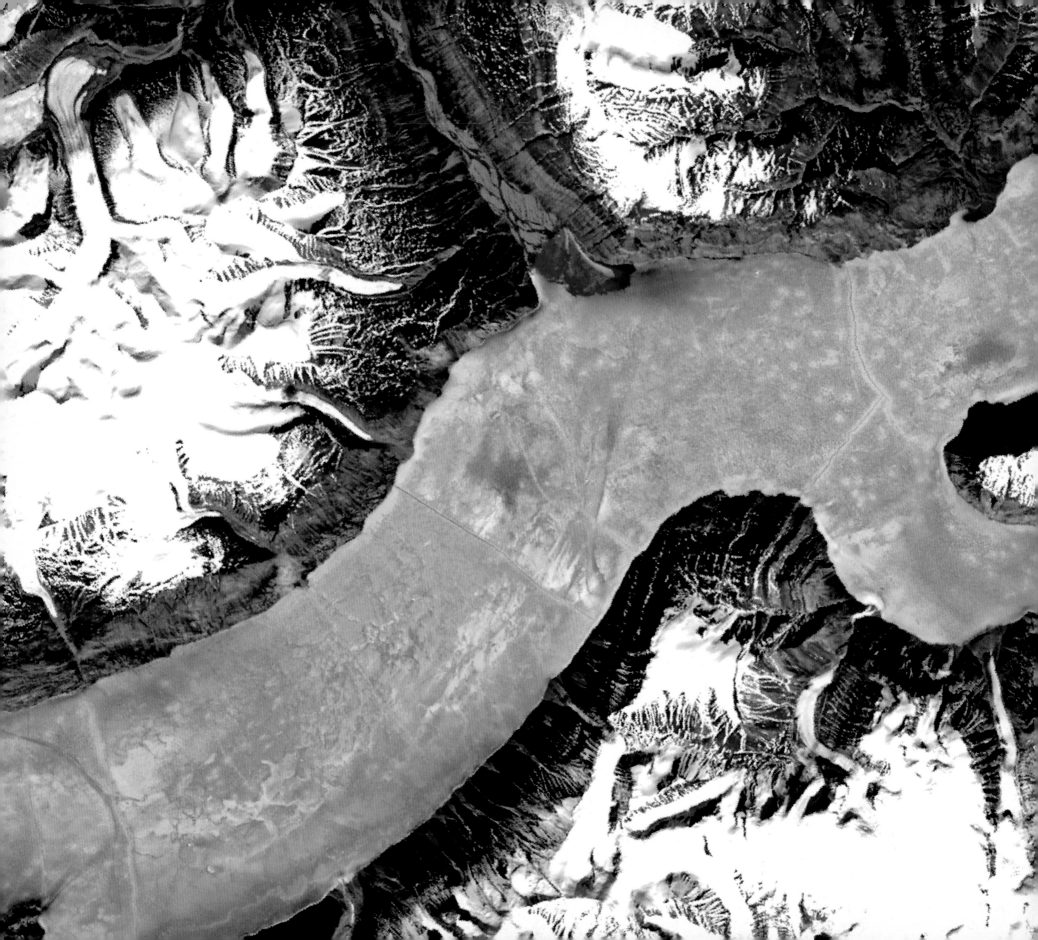

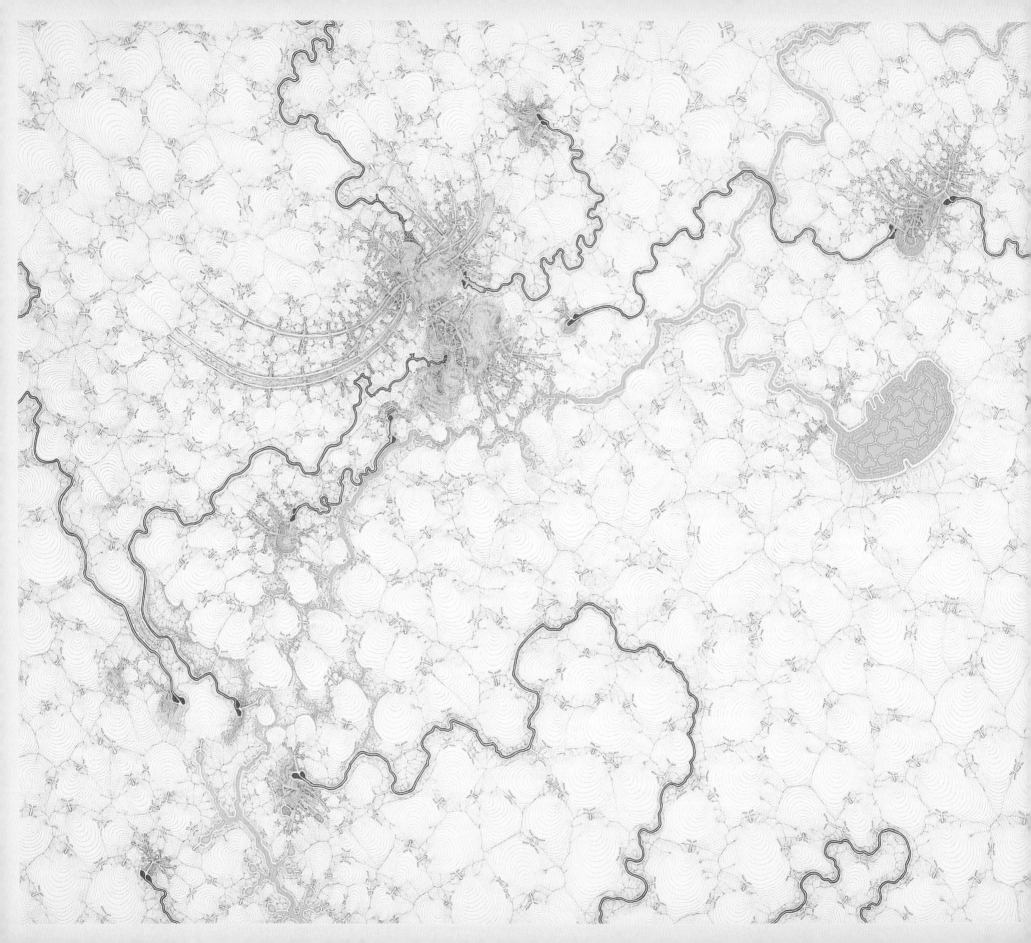

One should not despair of humanity or of progress: thanks to the political thaw of the late 20th century, new maps are appearing for the common good. Aside from the more than essential weather map that proves its usefulness daily by monitoring the rain, snow, fog, strong winds and beautiful weather, the experts have on their desks the scientific means to understand how, when and why the planet has been working the way it has since the beginning of time. We assign great ambitions to maps: to reveal that which remains invisible to the eye and is respectfully named using very precise words, such as soil moisture, muddiness of the water, night reflectance, remote sensing of suspended solids and the like. These codes are still unknown to laypeople because the earth, as seen from above, remains a true unknown. An improbable cameo of the color of fields in summer, the hatching of plowed fields, the meandering rivers and roads — cartographers relate on paper the results of these pictures taken from afar. Infrared removes the nuances, and the eye has to adapt so as not to confuse a grove with an oyster farm, a forest with a swamp or snowy rooftops with wheat fields. Everything becomes a great jumble for the amateur who does not know how to analyze the recent data. The most poetic among us, such the poet Paul Eluard, might shout "the Earth is blue like an orange." The hidden part of the world will always make us dream!

Nodular disparity (detail) by Daniel Zeller. (2006. Ink and acrylic on paper. 30 x 37 inches [76 x 94 cm].) (G-module Gallery, Paris.)

Bibliography

AUGÉ, Marc. *In the Metro*, trans. Tom Conley. Minneapolis: University of Minnesota Press, 2002.

AUJAC, Germaine. "Strabon et son temps," in *Geographie und verwandte Wissenschaften*, ed. Wolfgang Hübner. Stuttgart: Franz Steiner Verlag, 2000.

BALLAND, André. *La Terre mandarine*. Paris: Seuil, 1994.

BARIDON, Michel. *Naissance et renaissance du paysage*. Arles, France: Actes Sud, 2006.

BERLINSKI, David. *La Vie rêvée des maths*. Paris: Seuil, 2001.

BINGEN, Hildegard von. *Hildegard's Healing Plants: From Her Medieval Classic Physica*. Boston: Beacon Press, 2001.

BLACK, Jeremy. *Visions of the World: A History of Maps*. London: Mitchell Beazley, 2007.

BONNIOT DE RUISSELET, Jacques. *Le Nombril*. Paris: Seuil, 2000.

BOORSTIN, Daniel J. *The Discoverers*. New York: Vintage, 1985.

BOUGAINVILLE, Louis Antoine de. *A Voyage Round the World*. Cambridge, Massachusetts: Da Capo Press, 1967.

BOUVIER, Nicolas. *The Way of the World*, trans. Robyn Marsack. London: Eland & Sickle Moon Books, 2007.

BRUNET, Roger. *La Carte: Mode d'emploi*.

GUEDJ, Denis. *The Measure of the World: A Novel*, trans Arthur Goldhammer. Chicago: University of Chicago Press, 2001.

HALL, Edward T. *The Hidden Dimension*. New York: Anchor Books, 1990.

JARROSSON, Bruno. *Invitation à la philosophie des sciences*. Paris: Seuil, 1992.

JOLLY, Fernand. *La Cartographie*. Paris: Les Presses Universitaires de France, 1994.

JULLIEN, François. *The Propensity of Things: Toward a History of Efficacy in China*, trans. Janet Lloyd. Cambridge, Massachusetts: Zone Books, 1995.

KIRSH, Georges. *La Carte: Image des civilizations*. Paris: Seuil, 1980.

KI-ZERBO, Joseph. *Compagnons du soleil*. Paris: Éditions la Découverte, 1992.

LACHIÈZE-REY, Marc, and Jean-Pierre LUMINET. *Figures du ciel: De l'harmonie des sphères à la conquête spatiale*. Paris: Seuil/Bibliothèque National de France, 1998.

LE CLÉZIO, J.-M. G. *The Book of Flights: An Adventure Story*, trans. Simon Watson Taylor. New York: Atheneum, 1972.

LE GOFF, Jacques. *Héros et merveilles du Moyen Âge*. Paris: Éditions du Seuil, 2005.

LELIÈVRE, Dominique. *Voyageurs chinois à la découverte du monde*. Geneva: Éditions Olizane, 2004.

LINGS, Martin. *Muhammad: His Life Based on the Earliest Sources*. Rochester, Vermont: Inner Traditions, 2006.

LORICHON, Guy. *1099 Jérusalem conquise*. Paris: Seuil, 1998.

LUMINET, Jean-Pierre. *Atlas Coelestis*. Paris: Laboratoire Univers et Théories, Observatoire de Paris-Meudon.

MANGUEL, Alberto, and Giann GUADALUPI. *Dictionary of Imaginary Places: The Newly Updated and Expanded Classic*. Boston: Houghton Mifflin Harcourt, 2000.

MATHIEU, Rémi. *Anthologie des mythes et légendes de la chine anciennce*. Paris: Éditions Gallimard, 1989.

MONMONIER, Mark. *How to Lie with Maps*, 2nd ed. Chicago: University of Chicago Press, 1996.

MOREAU DEFARGES, Philippe. *Introduction à la géopolitique*. Paris: Seuil, 2005.

MORGAT, Alain. "Du Neptune françois au Pilote français: Les atlas nautiques avant 1850." Lecture, *Le livre maritime* conference, Brest, France, November 15–16, 2002.

NEYROLLES, Olivier. *La Lune*. Paris: Seuil, 1999.

OMONT, Sébstien. "La Piste des chants," *La Femelle du Requin* 6 (December 1996–January 1997).

PELLETIER, Monique. *Cartographie de la France et du monde de la Renaissance au siècle des Lumière*. Paris: Bibliothèque Nationale de la France, 2001.

PELLETIER, Monique, ed. *Couleurs de la Terre*. Paris: Seuil/BNF, 1998.

PERNOT, François. *Les Routes de la soie*. Paris: Artémis, 2001.

Ptolemy's Geography: An Annotated Translation of the Theoretical Chapters, trans. J. Lennart BERGGREN and Alexander JONES. Princeton, New Jersey: Princeton University Press, 2001.

RASHED, Roshi, ed. *Histoires des sciences arabes*. France: Seuil, 1997.

ROUX, Jean-Paul. *Les Explorateurs au Moyen Âge*. Paris: Seuil, 1961.

STENOU, Katérina. *Images de l'autre*. Paris: Seuil, 1998.

STRABO, *Geography*, trans. Horace L. Jones, 8 vols. Cambridge, Massachusetts: Harvard University Press, 1917–1932.

URBAIN, Jean-Didier. *L'Idiot du voyage: Histoires de touristes*. Paris: Payot, 1993.

VERDET, Jean-Pierre. *Voir et rêver le monde*. Paris: Larousse, 2002.

VERNANT, Jean-Pierre. *The Universe, the Gods and Men: Ancient Greek Myths*, trans. Linda Asher. New York: Harper Perennial, 2002.

VIGNAUX, Georges. *Du signe au virtuel: Les Nouveaux chemins de l'intelligence*. Paris: Seuil, 2003.

List of Maps

Photography Credits